"*The leaders of heretical sects...openly declared that, if the teaching of Thomas Aquinas were only taken away, they could easily battle with all Catholic teachers, gain the victory, and abolish the Church. A vain hope, indeed, but no vain testimony.*"

- POPE LEO XIII, AETERNI PATRIS

AQUINAS

ON REASONS FOR OUR FAITH

AGAINST THE MUSLIMS, AND A REPLY TO THE DENIAL OF PURGATORY BY CERTAIN GREEKS AND ARMENIANS: TO THE CANTOR OF ANTIOCH

BY ST. THOMAS AQUINAS

A Translation of
"DE RATIONIBUS FIDEI CONTRA SARACENOS, GRAECOS ET ARMENOS   ad Cantorem Antiochenum"

TRANSLATION BY

Fr. Peter Damian M. Fehlner, FI

EDITED, NOTATED AND INTRODUCED BY

James Likoudis

AQUINAS: On Reasons for Our Faith, is a booklet prepared for publication by the Franciscans of the Immaculate [marymediatrix.com], POB 3003, New Bedford, MA, 02741-3003.

Imprimatur   Most. Rev. Sean Patrick O'Malley
                 OFM Cap., Bishop of Fall River
                 Massachusetts, USA
                 October 4, 2002
                 Solemnity St. Francis of Assisi

The Imprimatur is a declaration of the Roman Catholic Church that the work is free from error in matters of faith and morals; but in no way does it imply that she endorses the contents of the work.

Front Cover: A picture of a life size image of the Angelic doctor St. Thomas Auqinas venerated at Our Lady's Chapel, New Bedford, MA

CONTENTS

The Glory of St. Thomas by Andrea di Bonaiuto. Florence - S. Maria Novella Capellone degli Spagnoli.

INTRODUCTION

ON REASONS FOR OUR FAITH AGAINST THE MUSLIMS, AND A REPLY TO THE DENIAL OF PURGATORY BY CERTAIN GREEKS AND ARMENIANS: *TO THE CANTOR OF ANTIOCH*

BY JAMES LIKOUDIS

St. Thomas Aquinas wrote his lengthy Letter "*De rationibus fidei contra Saracenos, Graecos et Armenos ad Cantorem Antiochenum*" about 1265 A.D. (1) soon after he had written his famous tract "*Contra errores Graecorum*" ("Against the Errors of the Greeks") (2) and his monumental "**Summa contra Gentiles**" ("Sum of the Truth of the Catholic Faith Against the Gentiles"). His response was in answer to the inquiries of a certain "Cantor of Antioch" (still unidentified) at the Latin cathedral in the city and who was in contact with Muslims (*Saracenos*) who ridiculed the Christian dogmas of the Trinity, Incarnation, Redemption, and the Holy Eucharist. In the ancient Christian city of Antioch there were also dissident Eastern Christians (Byzantine Greeks and Armenians) who had expressed their disbelief in Purgatory. He had also encountered other peoples (*alias nationes*) who shared with Muslims the denial of free will and merit.

The Angelic Doctor particularly notes to his correspondent who sought "moral and philosophical reasons" to convince the various opponents that the arguments sought are only effective on the basis of authorities accepted by them. While dissident Christians do accept the authority of the Scriptures, Muslims have to be approached with arguments solely from reason. St. Thomas takes care to observe that there are not "necessary reasons" which can prove the truth of articles of Catholic faith being questioned by Muslim "unbelievers"; rational arguments can only show such truths not to be contrary to reason. Supernatural truths exceed the powers of reason to demonstrate. In resolving the questions presented to him, St. Thomas explains how controversy with Muslim opponents should be conducted. His method of disputation he had explained even earlier in his *"Quod. IV q.9 a. 3"*:

> "A certain type of dispute is meant to dispel all doubt about the question of the existence of a 'given truth' [*an ita sit*], and therefore, in a theological discussion of this type, it is necessary to make use primarily of the authorities admitted by those with whom one is debating. If it is with Jews, we should make use of the authorities of the Old Testament; if it is the Manicheans, who reject the Old Testament, we should only use the authorities of the New Testament; if it is the schismatics, who admit the Old and New Testaments, but who reject the doctrine of our *sancti* [the Latin Fathers],

one will discuss with them in light of the two testaments and of those Fathers of the Church that they accept. If the adversary does not admit any of these authorities, then we will have recourse to rational arguments alone." (quoted in Jean-Pierre Torrell, O.P., *Saint Thomas Aquinas: Vol. I, The Person and the Work*, 1996, p. 124)

St. Thomas refers the Cantor of Antioch to his **Summa contra Gentiles** for a fuller treatment of the questions posed. It was in this **Summa** (requested by the Dominican Master General Raymond of Penafort to assist Dominican preachers in the apostolate with Muslims) that the Saint refuted the philosophical and theological errors of such noted Muslim scholars as Ibn-Sima (Avicenna 980-1037), Ibn-Gabirol (Avicebron c. 1021-1058), and Ibn-Rushd (Averroes 1126-1198). Much of the apologetics found in that great work may be said to constitute reflections on the philosophy of religion shared in some measure by both Christians and Muslims.

In his "Reasons for Our Faith Against the Muslims, Greeks and Armenians: to the Cantor of Antioch", St. Thomas explains for Muslims the meaning of the term "*Generation*", clarifies the meaning of "*Procession*", and gives the reasons for the Incarnation of the Word, the Eternal Son of God. He explains at some length how the words "God was made man" are to be understood as well as the expression "The Word of God suffered." After proceeding to deal with objections to the doctrine of the Holy Eucharist, he proceeds to refute the arguments of dissident Greeks and Armenians against the doctrine of Purgatory. Towards the end of this little work, the Angelic Doctor shows that the theory of predestination does not involve God's imposing any necessity on human acts.

As the Catholic Church engages in the evangelization of the modern world, it will continue to follow the way outlined in Vatican II's *"Nostra Aetate"*, ("Declaration on the Relation of the Church to Non-Christian Religions, October 28, 1965) noting with regards to Islam:

"The Church has also a high regard for the Muslims. They worship God, who is one, living and subsistent, merciful and almighty, the Creator of heaven and earth, who has also spoken to men. They strive to submit themselves to the hidden decrees of God, just as Abraham submitted himself to God's plan, to whose faith Muslims eagerly link their own. Although not acknowledging him as God, they venerate Jesus as a prophet, his Virgin Mother they also honor, and even at times devoutly invoke. Further, they await the day of judgment and the reward of God following the resurrection of the dead. For this reason they highly esteem an upright life and worship God, especially by way of prayer, alms-deeds and fasting.

Over the centuries many quarrels and dissensions have arisen between Christians and Muslims. The sacred Council now pleads with all to forget the past, and urges that a sincere effort be made to achieve mutual understanding; for the benefit of all men, let them preserve and promote peace, liberty, social jus-

tice and moral values." (no. 3) (A. Flannery,O.P., Vatican Council II, The Conciliar and Post-Conciliar Documents, 1981 Edition, pp. 739-40)

It is evident that the Catholic Church does not hesitate to appreciate the positive elements in Islam which stem from the influence of both Judaism and Christianity. Catholics are called upon to appreciate the spiritual patrimony common to both the Church and Islam, and to overcome the psychological and cultural obstacles which are the heritage of former centuries of hostility and violent confrontation (witnessed by 14 Crusades on the one hand and marked on the other hand by a continuing oppression and persecution of Christians in Muslim countries). When Pope John Paul II entered the Umayyed Mosque in Damascus, Syria, he may be said to have turned a new page in the mixed history of Catholic-Muslim relations, seeking dialogue on all levels, including the theological.

With respect to the positive theological elements contained in Islam, Catholics find that the Muslim's sacred book, the Qur'an, itself affirms the...

Existence of one transcendent God;
The existence of angels and demons;
Christ as Messiah, prophet and messenger of God;

The Virginal birth and sinlessness of the son of Mary (she who "was chosen above all women");

Reality of his miracles including the raising of the dead to life;

Christ's being Allah's 'Word';

His mysterious Ascension to God in heaven;

His return at the end of time;

His defeat of the Antichrist;

Everlasting life in heaven or hell.

For devout Muslims, Jesus is a model of true Islam, or total submission to God. Nevertheless, there remains the denial of the Trinity and Divinity of Christ which are believed to contradict the unity and majesty of God. As a Catholic scholar has noted,

"The Qur'an recognizes Jesus as a 'word from Allah' (3:45), and as "strengthened with the Holy Spirit" (2:87) but denies the Son and the Holy Spirit as distinct divine persons, nor does it view Allah as Father in the proper sense of the word." (Roch Kereszty, O.Cist., "*A Catholic Perspective in Dialogue with Judaism and Islam*", Communio, Fall 2000).

Catholic apologists have also noted Muslim denials that Christ was crucified and resurrected from the dead, truths which also lie at the very heart of the Christian Faith.

It remains that few Muslims have a real understanding of Christianity, and St. Thomas' "*De rationibus fidei…*" as well as his other works remain valuable for meeting the serious misconceptions and errors Muslims have of the Christian Faith. His writings in defense of the Catholic Faith retain their value for the future theological dialogue with

Muslims. In view of Vatican II's emphasis on the beliefs that Muslims share with Christians, modern readers may perhaps find surprising St. Thomas' use of the term "unbelievers" with respect to Muslims. This was a feature of the medieval Christian polemic against Muslim denials of revealed truths in the context of a militant Islam engaged in military and ideological expansionism against both Latin and Byzantine Christendoms. As another Catholic scholar has pointed out, "While Aquinas embodies the polemical and critical attitude that many medieval Christians had towards Islam, there are examples of a more irenic approach." (Dr. Robert L. Fastiggi, "*The Incarnation: Muslim Objections and the Christian Response*", The Thomist, 57, 3, July 1993)

NOTES

(1) This translation of St. Thomas Aquinas' "*De rationibus fidei contra Saracenos, Graecos et Armenos ad Cantorem Antiochenum*" has been made from the Leonine edition of his works, vol. 40, B pp. 57-73. A literal translation of this work has been preferred as the clearest way of communicating the mind and theological method of the great Scholastic.

The only other English translation of the entire work is Fr. Joseph Kenny, O.P.'s annotated translation which appears in "*Islamochristiana*" (Rome 1996), which was unavailable for purposes of comparison at the time of this publication. An English translation of Chapter V in "*De rationibus fidei*" by H. Nash, "Why Did God the Son Become Man?" appeared in *Life of the Spirit*, London, Blackfriars, 1952.

2) A complete translation of St. Thomas Aquinas' "*Contra errors Graecorum*" by Fr. Peter Damian Fehlner, FFI, is found in my "Ending the Byzantine Greek Schism" (1992) (available from : James Likoudis, P.O.Box 852, Montour Falls, N.Y. 14865- $17.95- includes S&H). The same volume contains Fr. Fehlner's translations of St. Peter Damian's *Letter on the Procession of the Holy Spirit to the patriarch of Constantinople, Constantine III Lichoudes (*c. 1061 A.D.) and the *Letter to the Abbot and Monks of a Greek monastery* by the Dominican friar John de Fontibus, O.P. (1350 A.D.).

The Chastity of St. Thomas by Velasquez. Museo Diocesano, Orihuela. Thomas had a vision of two angels who presented him with the cord of chastity.

THOMAS AQUINAS

DE RATIONIBUS FIDEI CONTRA SARACENOS,
GRAECOS ET ARMENOS   ad Cantorem Antiochenum

ON REASONS FOR OUR FAITH AGAINST THE
MUSLIMS, AND A REPLY TO THE DENIAL OF
PURGATORY BY CERTAIN GREEKS AND
ARMENIANS: *TO THE CANTOR OF ANTIOCH*

Translation by
Fr. Peter Damian Fehlner, FI

CHAPTER ONE

THE AUTHOR'S INTENTION

Blessed Peter the Apostle, who received from the Lord the promise that on his confession of faith would be built the Church against which the Gates of Hell could not prevail and that against these Gates of Hell the faith entrusted to him would continue inviolate (Cf. Mt. 16:18), addressed the faithful saying: *"Sanctify the Lord Christ in your hearts"* (1 Pet. 3:15), that is, through the firmness of faith. On this foundation placed in our heart we will be able to stand safe against all attack or mockery of unbelievers [*infidelium*] whence he adds: *"being ready always to satisfy everyone that asks you a reason of that hope which is in you."*

Christian faith, however, principally consists in the confession of the Holy Trinity and especially boasts in the Cross of Our Lord Jesus Christ, *"For the word of the cross, as Paul says, "is foolishness; but to them that are saved, that is, to us, it is the power of God."* (1 Cor. 1:18) Our hope, too, consists in two things, namely, in that which we await after death and in the help of God by which in this life we are aided in meriting future bliss through works freely performed.

These, then, are the points, which, as you affirm, are attacked and ridiculed by the unbelievers. For the Muslims [*Saraceni*], as you say, ridicule our claim that Christ is the Son of God, since God does not have a wife [cf. the Qur'an VI, 110; 72: 3]; and they think us mad, assuming we profess there are three gods. They also mock our belief that Christ, the Son of God, was crucified for the salvation of the human race [cf. Qur'an 4: 157-8], because if God is omnipotent, He could have saved the human race without the suffering of His own Son; He could also have so constructed man that he could not have sinned. They rebuke Christians because daily at the altar they eat their God and because the body of Christ, were it even as big as a mountain, should long since have been consumed.

Concerning the state of souls after death you state that the Greeks (1) and Armenians err when they claim that until the Day of Judgment souls are neither punished nor rewarded (2), but are, as it were, sequestered because they ought not to have either punishment or reward without their bodies; and in support of their error they cite what the Lord says in the Gospel: *"In My Father's house there are many mansions."* (John 14:2)

About merits which depend on free will you state that on grounds of divine foreknowledge and decree both the Muslims and other nations (3) ascribe to human acts a kind of necessity, such that man cannot die or even sin, except as God decrees this of man, and that each person has his fate inscribed on his forehead. (4)

On these points you request moral and philosophical reasons (5) which the Muslims might consider; for it would be fruitless to cite authorities against persons who do not recognize them. Wishing, therefore, to comply with your request which appears to stem from a holy desire, so that you might be ready according to the apostolic teaching (cf. 1 Pet. 3:15) to satisfy everyone asking you a reason, I will explain for you, to the extent their content is pertinent to the foregoing, several easier themes elsewhere (6) treated by me at greater length.

CHAPTER TWO

HOW ONE IS TO DISPUTE *WITH UNBELIEVERS* [INFIDELES] (7)

There is one matter about which I want to advise you, namely, when you dispute with unbelievers about the articles of faith, you should not try to prove the faith with necessary reasons, for such a procedure would deprive the faith of its sublime quality, the truth of which not only transcends human minds, but angelic as well. These, in fact, are believed by us as revealed by God. Because whatever proceeds from the Supreme Truth cannot be false, nor can anything necessarily true be used successfully to attack what is not false, our faith cannot be proven by necessary reasons. Neither, moreover, can it be disproved by necessary reasons, and this is precisely because of its truth.

To this, therefore, must be directed the intention of a Christian disputing about the articles of faith, not in order to prove the Faith, but to defend it. Hence Blessed Peter does not say "ready always to prove" but rather "*to satisfy*" (1 Pet. 3:15), namely that it might reasonably be shown that what Catholic faith confesses is not false.

CHAPTER THREE

HOW GENERATION IN THE GODHEAD IS TO BE UNDERSTOOD (8)

First, therefore, consideration should be given to the silly character of the ridicule heaped by Muslims upon our assertion that Christ is the Son of God, as though God is thereby said to have a wife. For since the mockers are carnal, they are incapable of grasping anything except what pertains to flesh and blood. Anyone of intelligence, however, can realize that the process of begetting is not the same in all things, but occurs in each thing according to its own proper characteristics. Thus, in some animals it occurs through male and female intercourse; in plants, however, through sprouting or germination, and otherwise in others. Now God is not of a carnal nature, such that He needs intercourse with a woman so as to beget, but is of a spiritual or intellectual nature; rather He is above every intellect. Hence generation in Him is to be understood in the manner appropriate to an intellectual nature. And although our intellect falls short of the perfection of the divine, we nonetheless cannot otherwise speak of the divine intellect except in terms of a likeness to what we find in our own intellect.

Our intellect, however, sometimes understands potentially, sometimes actually. Now, as often as it understands something in act, it forms something which is, as it were, its offspring. For this reason it is called a mental concept. And indeed this is what is signified by the voice outwardly. Hence, as the voice conveying meaning is said to be the outer word, so the inner concept of the mind signified by the outer word is called the intellectual or mental word.

This concept of our mind, however, is not the very essence of our mind, but a kind of accident inhering in it, because our understanding itself is not the very being of our intellect. Otherwise our intellect would never for a moment be without understanding in actual fact.

The word, therefore, of our intellect can be termed either a concept or offspring by virtue of a certain analogy, especially when our intellect understands itself, in so far, namely, as there issues a certain likeness of the intellect proceeding from its capacity to understand, just as a son proceeding from his father's power to beget bears his father's likeness.

But in the proper sense our intellectual word cannot be called a concept or offspring, because it does not have the same nature as our intellect. Not all proceeding from another, even if similar to that other, is called a son. Otherwise the self-portrait of a painter would have to be called his son. For to be a son it is necessary that the one proceeding have both the likeness of him from whom he proceeds and be of the same nature with him.

But because in God understanding is naught other than His very Being, it follows that the word which is conceived in His intellect is neither some accident nor something foreign to His nature; by the very fact that it is a word it has the character of one proceeding from another, such that it also be the likeness of the One whose word it is. This, of course, is also found in our word.

But further that divine word is such as to be not some accident, not some part of God who is simple, not something foreign to the divine nature, but something complete subsisting in the divine nature, having the character of one proceeding from another. For without this that divine word could not be understood to be a word. This, however, according to the conventions of human speech is called a son, because a son proceeds from another according to the likeness of that other, subsisting in the same nature with Him.

In so far, then, as the divine can be described in human terms, we call the word of the divine intellect the Son of God; the God, however, whose is the word, we call the Father; and the procession of the word we term the generation of the Son, immaterial indeed, not carnal as carnal men are inclined to suppose.

There is, moreover, another point on which the aforementioned generation of the Son of God differs from every other human generation , whether the material one whereby man is born of man, or the intelligible one whereby a word is conceived in the human mind. For in both instances that which proceeds by generation exists in time subsequently to that from which it proceeds. For a father does not beget immediately from the start of his existence, but must pass from an imperfect state in which he is able to beget; nor again is a son born immediately at the inception of the generative process, because carnal generation consists in a certain change and succession. In the intellectual realm, too, man is not immediately ready to form intellectual concepts; and even after he has reached that degree of maturity he does not always understand in act, but first understands only in potency and afterwards in act. And he can also cease to understand in act and continue to understand only in potency and habitually.

In this way, therefore, the word of man is consequent in time to man himself, and sometimes ceases to be before the man does. It is, however, impossible that such like be found in God, in whom neither imperfection nor change of any kind has place, nor any kind of passage from potency to act since He is Pure Act and First Act. The word of God, then, is coeternal with God Himself.

There is still another point at which our word differs from the Divine Word. For our intellect does not understand all things simultaneously, nor by a single act, but with many, and so the words of our intellect are many. But God understands all things simultaneously and by a single act, because His understanding cannot be but one with His very Being. Hence it follows that in God there is only one Word.

There is a final difference to be considered, namely that the word of our intellect does not match the potential of the intellect, because when we conceive something mentally we can still conceive many other things. Hence, the word of our intellect is both imperfect and subject to composition when from several perfect words is made one more perfect, as when the intellect conceives the enunciation or definition of something. But the Divine Word fully matches the power of God, because God through His essence understands Himself, and all else. Hence as great as is His essence, so great is the Word which by His essence He conceives understanding Himself and all else. It is, therefore, perfect and simple and equal to God.

And for the reason just mentioned this Word we call the Son of God. Of the same nature as the Father we confess Him the Father's coeternal, only-begotten and perfect Son.

CHAPTER FOUR

HOW WITHIN THE GODHEAD THE PROCESSION OF THE HOLY SPIRIT FROM THE FATHER AND THE SON IS TO BE UNDERSTOOD (9)

It is to be observed, further, how some appetitive action follows on all knowing. Among all the various appetitive activities, however, love is found to be the principal (10), which, if missing, there be neither joy when someone acquires what he does not love, nor sadness if impeded from what he does not love. When love is absent, then as a consequence all other appetitive activities in one way or another referred to sadness and joy are absent. Since, then, in God there is most perfect knowledge, it is also necessary to predicate of Him perfect love. In such love by virtue of an appetitive operation, just as in the word by virtue of an intellectual operation, a procession is expressed.

But a certain difference between an operation of the intellect and of the appetite is to be noticed. For an intellectual operation, indeed any cognitive act, is brought to term when what is knowable in some way comes to exist in the knower, as for instance the sensible in the senses and the intelligible in the intellect. An appetitive operation, however, is brought to term according to a certain order or movement of the appetite toward the objects presented to it. Now whatever constitutes the hidden origin of its activity receives the name of spirit. For winds are thus called spirits, because the origin of their blowing is not apparent; respiration, too, and the circulation of the arteries proceeding from an interior and hidden source take the name of spirit. Appropriately, then, in so far as the divine can be signified by human terms, divine love in proceeding takes the name of Spirit.

But in us love proceeds from a double source: sometimes from corporeal and material nature, which often enough is an unclean love because through it the purity of our mind is disturbed; sometimes, however, from the distinctive character of our nature's spirit, as when we love intelligible goods and those in conformity with our reason. This love is pure. In God, however, material love has no place. Appropriately, therefore, we call His love of Himself not only Spirit, but Holy Spirit, so that in terming that Spirit Holy His purity is expressed.

It is evident, however, that we can love nothing with an intelligible and holy love except to the degree we conceive in act (11) intellectually. Now, a concept of the intellect is a word; hence, it is necessary that love arises from a word. The Word of God, however, we call the Son; whence it is clear the Holy Spirit is from the Son.

But just as the divine understanding is His Being; so also the Love of God is His very Being. And as God always understands in act and to understand all things understands Himself, so too He always loves in act and loves all things by loving His own goodness. As therefore the Son of God who is the Word of God subsists in the divine nature, is coeternal with the Father, is the perfect and only Son, so all this must be confessed of the Holy Spirit as well.

From all this, then, we can gather that, since anything subsisting in an intelligent nature is called by us a *person,* by the Greeks a *hypostasis* (12), it is necessary to say that the Word of God, whom we name the Son of God, is a hypostasis or person; and likewise this must be said of the Holy Spirit. For no one has any doubt that God from whom the Word and Love proceed is something subsisting, such that He can also be called a hypostasis or person. And in this way we appropriately posit in God three persons, namely, the person of the Father, the person of the Son, the person of the Holy Spirit.

But we do not assert that these three hypostases or persons differ essentially, because, as said above (13), as the understanding and love of God are His very Being, so His Word and Love are the very essence of God. Whatever is predicated of God absolutely, however, is nothing other than the essence of God. For God is not great or powerful or good accidentally, but by His essence. Hence, we do not say the three persons or hypostases are differentiated by anything absolute, but only by virtue of the relations which arise from the procession of the Word and of Love. And because we term the procession of the Word a generation, and relations of paternity and filiation originate from a generation, we say the person of the Son is distinguished from the person of the Father only by paternity and filiation, thus predicating all else of both in common and equally. For just as we say the Father is true God, omnipotent, eternal, and so with whatever else is similarly predicated, so also the Son ; and the same for the Holy Spirit.

Because, therefore, the Father and the Son and the Holy Spirit are not distinguished by reason of the divine nature, but by the relations alone, quite appropriately we do not say there are three Gods, but confess one true and perfect God. With men, however, three persons are called three men and not one man, precisely because human nature which is common to the three belongs to each differently by reason of their material division, something having absolutely no place in God. Hence, since in three men there are three humanities numerically distinct, only the form of humanity is common to all. But in the three divine persons there are not three divinities numerically distinct; rather there is, necessarily, only one simple Deity, since the essence of the Word and of Love in God is not other than the essence of God. And so we confess not three Gods, but one God because of the one, simple Deity in three persons.

CHAPTER FIVE

WHAT WAS THE REASON FOR THE INCARNATION OF THE SON OF GOD? (14)

From a similar mental blindness Muslims are led to ridicule as well the Christian Faith which confesses Christ, the Son of God, died, because they do not grasp the depth of so great a mystery. And lest the death of the Son of God be understood perversely, first something must be said about the Incarnation of the Son of God. For we do not assert that the Son of God was subject to death by virtue of the divine nature in which He is equal to the Father, a nature which is the source of all life, but by virtue of our nature which He assumed in the unity of the person.

In order, then, to arrive at a balanced appreciation of the mystery of the divine Incarnation, one must observe how every worker goes about his tasks by way of the agent intellect and the concept of his intellect which we call a word, as is clear in the case of the builder and of any artist who is outwardly productive according to a form which he conceives mentally. Because, therefore, the Son of God is the very Word of God, it follows that God made all things through His Son.

Each thing, however, comes to be and is repaired by the same factors. For should a house have fallen, it is repaired according to the art form whereby it was erected initially. Among the creatures, however, created by God through His Word, the rational creature holds preeminent place, in so far as all other creatures serve him and appear to be subordinated to him. And reasonably so, for only the rational creature has control over his own acts in virtue of free will. Other creatures, however, do no act by virtue of free discretion, but are constrained to act by force of nature. Now everywhere what is free holds preeminence over what is servile: servants are bound to serve the free and are governed by the free. By any fair standard, therefore, the fall of the rational creature can only be assessed as greater than a defect of any irrational creature. Nor is there any doubt that divine judgment nests fair standards. Hence, it is above all fitting for Divine Wisdom to repair the fall of the rational creature, even more than to repair the heavens should they fall or anything else which corporeal things might suffer.

Now, there are two rational or intellectual creatures: one existing apart from a body which creature we call an angel, the other united to a body which creature is the soul of man. In both, however, a fall could have occurred because of free will. I say the fall of a rational creature, not in the sense of failing to be, but in the sense of failing in rectitude of will. For a fall or defect is primarily defined in terms of that by which any agent acts, as when we say an artist errs if he is deficient in the art by which he works. And we say a natural agent is defective and fallen if the natural power by which it acts is corrupted, as for example, if in a plant the power to germinate should be defective or in the earth the power to fructify. That, however, in virtue of which the rational creature acts is the will. Freedom is distinctive of the will. The fall, then, of a rational creature occurs in so far as it falls away from the rectitude of the will, which is effected by sin. Hence, it is primarily fitting for God to remove the defect of sin, which is nothing other than the perversity of the will, and this through His Word through whom He created every rational creature.

In fact, the sin of the angels could have no remedy, because in virtue of the immutability of their nature they are incapable of repenting of anything, once they have turned to it. Men, however, because of the condition of their nature have a will which is changeable, such that not only can they choose diverse goods or evils, but even after they have chosen one they can repudiate it and turn to some other. And this mutability of man's will remains, so long as it is united to a body subject to variation. When, however, the soul will have been separated from this kind of body, it will have the same immutability as the angel naturally has. Hence, the human soul after death will also be incapable of repentance ; it can neither turn from good to evil nor from evil to good. Therefore, for this reason it befitted God's goodness that He repair a fallen human nature through His Son.

The manner, however, of reparation had to be such as would be appropriate both to the nature to be repaired and to its disease. I say to the nature to be repaired, because, since man's is a rational nature endowed with free will, he was to be recalled to the state of righteousness not by necessity of outer force, but through his own will; to the disease as well because, since the disease consisted in the perversity of the will, the reparation had to be effected by returning the will to righteousness. The righteousness of the human will, however, consists in the ordering of love which is its principal affection. An orderly love, however, consists in this : that we love God above everything as the supreme good and that all else we love be referred to Him as to its last end, and that also in loving other things a right order be observed, such that we prefer the spiritual to bodily goods.

Now, nothing could be more effective in stimulating our love for God than that the Word of God, through whom all things were made, should for the reparation of our nature assume it, such that the same person might be God and man. And first, because by this is most effectively proven how much God loves man that He would become man for his salvation ; nor does anything so stimulate to love more than that anyone should know himself to be loved.

Next, because man having his understanding and affection lowered to corporeal things, could not easily be lifted to things beyond him. It is easy, however, for any man to love and to know another man, but to consider the sublimity of God and to be lifted up to it by the requisite, loving affection is not something any man can do, but only those who by the help of God with great effort and work are raised from corporeal things to spiritual. Therefore, that an easy way to God might open to all men, God willed to become man, that even little children might think of and love

God as one like themselves, and so through that which they are able to grasp they might little by little progress toward the perfect.

Also, by the fact that God became man, hope is given man that he can also come to share in that perfect bliss which God alone naturally possesses. For, should it be promised him that he might attain a happiness of which the angels are hardly capable, which consists, namely, in the vision and enjoyment of God, man realizing his infirmity would hardly be able to hope for this, unless on the other hand there be shown to him the dignity of human nature, which God so greatly esteemed that He willed to become man for his salvation. And so by the fact that God became man He has given to us hope that we also might be able to attain this: to be united to God through blessed enjoyment.

Realizing his own dignity from the fact that God assumed human nature is also effective for man unto this that he should not permit his affection to be enslaved to any creature, neither by worshiping idolatrously demons or any other creatures, nor by disorderly love subjecting himself to bodily creatures. For in as much as man is of such dignity according to God's estimation and so near God that God willed to become man, it is unworthy of man to subject himself by disorderly conduct to things inferior to God.

CHAPTER SIX

HOW THE SAYING, GOD WAS MADE MAN, MUST BE UNDERSTOOD (15)

When, however, we say that God was made man, let no one think this is to be understood as though God were changed into man, as air becomes fire when turned into fire. For the nature of God is immutable ; bodies rather are what are changed into each other. A spiritual nature, however, is not changed into a corporeal one, but can in some fashion be united to it through its own power to act, as the soul to the body. And although human nature is composed of soul and body, the soul nonetheless is not of a corporeal, but of a spiritual nature. Every spiritual creature, however, falls far shorter of the divine simplicity than any corporeal creature of the simplicity of a spiritual nature. As, therefore, a spiritual nature is united to a body through its own power to act, so also God can be united both to a spiritual and to a bodily nature. And in this way we say God was united to human nature.

Now, it is to be noted that each thing seems most of all to be what in it is considered preeminent. All else, however, appears to adhere to whatever is preeminent and to be assumed by it, in so far as that which is preeminent uses all else according to its good pleasure. Indeed this is evident not only in civil assemblies, in which the princes of the city appear to enclose, as it were, the entire city(16) and to employ, according to their own dispositions, everyone else as though members adhering to them and as naturally joined to them. For, although man consists of soul and body, nonetheless man appears primarily to be soul to which a body adheres, and which is used by the soul for appropriate activities. So also, then, in the union of God to a creature the divinity is not drawn into the human nature, rather the human nature is assumed by God ; not indeed that it might be changed into God, but that it might adhere to God, and that in some way the soul and body thus assumed might be the body and soul of God Himself, as the parts of the body assumed by the soul are in some way members of its soul.

In this, nevertheless, there is another difference to be noticed. For the soul, although it be more perfect than the body, nonetheless does not possess in itself the total perfection of human nature. Hence, the body so comes to it that from soul and body is formed one human nature whose several parts are soul and body. But God is so perfect in His own nature that nothing can be added to the fullness of His nature. Hence, the divine nature cannot thus be united to another so that from both there is formed one common nature, for thus the divine nature would be a part of that common nature. This contradicts the perfection of the divine nature, for a part by definition is imperfect. God, therefore, the Word of God, so assumed a human nature which is composed of soul and body in such a way that one nature did not pass into the other nor was one nature conflated out of two. Rather, after the union the two natures remained distinct, each retaining its own natural properties.

Consideration, moreover, is to be given the fact that, since a spiritual nature is united to a bodily nature through its spiritual power, the greater the power of a spiritual nature, the more perfectly and durably it assumes a nature inferior to itself. Infinite, however, is God's power to which every creature is subject, and He uses each according to His discretion. But He does not use them unless in some wise by His power to act He is united to them. He is, then, more perfectly united to any created nature exactly in proportion to the degree He more fully exercises His power on it. Now He exercises His power on all creatures in this regard that He bestows existence on all and moves them to their proper activities, and accordingly He is said to be in all things in some common way. But in some more special way He exercises His power in holy minds, which He not only conserves in existence and moves to act as with other creatures, but turns them to the knowledge and love of Himself. Hence, He is also said to dwell in holy minds in a special way and holy minds are said to be full of God.

Because, therefore, God is said to be united more or less to a creature according to the quantity of power which He exercises on the creature, it is obvious that, since the effectiveness of the divine power cannot be comprehended by the human intellect, God can be united to a creature in a way far sublimer than anything the human intellect can understand. Hence, we say that in some incomprehensible and ineffable (17) way God was united to a human nature in Christ not only by inhabitation as with the other saints, but in some unique way, such that this human nature would be a nature of the Son of God ; that the Son of God who from eternity has the divine nature from the Father, in time through this wondrous assumption, has a human nature of our race. And thus any parts of this human nature can be predicated of the very Son of God, and whatever any part of this human nature does or suffers can be ascribed to the only-begotten Word of God. Hence, not inappropriately, we say that both the soul and body, and even the eyes and hands are those of the Son of God ; and that the Son of God sees corporeally by virtue of ocular vision, and hears by virtue of auricular hearing : and so, too, for anything else which may be fitting either to the parts of the soul or of the body.

Of this wondrous union, however, no more appropriate example can be found than that of the union of a body and a rational soul. It is an especially fitting example of the fact that the word which remains hidden in the heart becomes sensible by being vocalized and written. Nonetheless, these examples fall far short in the representation of the aforesaid union, just as other human examples as well in regard to divine things. For neither is the divinity so united as to become part of another composite, as the soul is a part of human nature ; nor is it so united to a human nature as merely to be signified by it, as the word of the heart is signified by sounds or by writing, but in such wise that the Son of God truly has a human nature and is called man. Hence, it is clear that we do not so claim God to be united to a corporeal nature that He is a power in the body after the manner of material things and corporeal powers, because not even the intellect (18) of the soul so united to a body is a power of the body. Much less, then, is the Word of God who in an ineffable and more sublime way assumed to Himself a human nature.

On the basis of the foregoing it is, therefore, clear that the Son of God has both a divine nature and a human nature, one from eternity, the other in time by an assumption. Now it happens that many things are possessed by the same subject in diverse manners, in all of which, nonetheless, that which enjoys preeminence is always said to have (or possess) the other, but that which is secondary is always said to be had (or possessed) by the first. For a whole has many parts, as a man has hands and feet ; we do not say contrariwise that hands and feet have a man. One subject also has many accidents, as an apple color and smell, and not contrariwise. Man also has certain externals, such as possessions and clothing, and not contrariwise.

In only those things, however, which are parts of some one thing, is anything said to have and be had, as the soul has a body and a body has a soul. And in so far as man and wife are joined in one marriage, the man is said to have a wife and the wife a husband. Likewise in other matters united by relation, as when we say that a father has a son and a son a father. If, therefore, God were so united to human nature as a soul to a body, that from this union one common nature were formed, it could be said that God has a human nature and a human nature has God, as a soul has a body and vice-versa. But because from the divine and human natures one nature cannot be constituted on account of the perfection of the divine nature, as already said (19), yet in the aforesaid union the preeminent factor is located on the side of the divine, it obviously follows that what is said to have a human nature is to be found in the area of the divine.

That, however, which has a nature of any kind is said to be the supposit (subject) (20) or hypostasis of that nature, as that which has the nature of a horse is said to be a hypostasis or supposit. And if the nature had should be intellectual, such a hypostasis will be called a person, for example when we say Peter is a person because he has a human nature which is an intellectual nature. Since, therefore, the Son of God, the only-begotten Word of God, through its assumption has a human nature as already said (21), it follows that He is the supposit (subject), hypostasis or person of that human nature. And since from eternity He has a divine nature, not by way of composition, but of simple identity, He is also called the hypostasis or person of the divine nature, to the extent divine matters can be expressed in human words. Hence, the only-begotten Word of God Himself is the hypostasis or person of the two natures, the divine namely and the human, subsisting in these two natures.

Should, however, anyone object that, since human nature in Christ is not an accident, but a definite substance-not a universal, rather a particular one which is termed a hypostasis-, it seems to follow that this very human nature in Christ is a hypostasis over and above the hypostasis of the Word of God, and so in Christ there are two hypostases. However, such an objector must consider that not every particular substance is called a hypostasis, but only that which is not possessed by some more preeminent one. For the human hand is a definite, particular substance, but still it is not said to be a hypostasis or person because it is possessed by one more preeminent substance which is man ; otherwise there would be in man as many hypostases or persons as there are members or parts. The human nature in Christ, therefore, is not an accident, but a substance- not universal, but particular-; nevertheless, it cannot be called a hypostasis, because it is assumed by something more preeminent, namely, the Word of God.

So, therefore, Christ is one by reason of a unity of person or hypostasis ; nor can Christ properly be said to be two persons ; rather Christ is properly said to have two natures. And although the divine nature is predicated of the hypostasis of Christ, which is the hypostasis of the Word of God, which is His very own essence, nonetheless the human nature cannot be predicated of Him in the abstract, as it cannot be predicated of anyone having a human nature. For just as we cannot say that Peter is human nature, but that he is a man to the extent that he has human nature, so we cannot say that the Word of God is a human nature, but rather that He has taken on a human nature, and so He is called a man.

Each nature, therefore, (22) is predicated of the Word of God : but only one concretely, namely, the human, as when we say "the Son of God is man", whereas the divine nature is predicated abstractly and concretely. For it can be said that the Word of God is the divine essence or nature, and that He is God. Since, however, God is someone having a divine nature and man someone having a human nature, by these two terms are connoted the two natures possessed, but only one person possesses both. And because someone possessing is a hypostasis, just as in the term God is understood the hypostasis of the Word of God, so in the term man is understood the hypostasis of the Word of God, to the extent this is ascribed to Christ. And so it is clear that when we say Christ is God and man, we do not say that He is two persons, but one in two natures, nevertheless.

Because, however, whatever is fitting to a nature can be ascribed to the hypostasis of that nature, and the hypostasis both of the human nature and of the divine nature is included both in the term connoting the divine nature and in the term connoting the human, precisely because it is the same hypostasis having both natures : consequently both the divine and the human are predicated of that hypostasis, either in so far as it is included in the term connoting the divine nature, or in so far as it is included in the term connoting the human nature. Thus, we can say that God, the Word of God, was conceived and born of the Virgin, suffered, died and was buried, ascribing to the hypostasis of the Word of God human properties by reason of His human nature. And conversely we can say that this man is one with the Father, and that He is from eternity and that He created the world, by reason of the divine nature.

Hence, in considering these so diverse predicates of Christ are ascribed to Christ, one distinguishes: some are predicated by reason of the human nature, some by reason of the divine nature. But on considering the one of whom they are predicated, they are affirmed without differentiation, because the hypostasis of which the divine and the human natures are predicated is the same. For instance, if I say that the man who sees and hears is the same, but not by reason of the same, for he sees with his eyes and hears with his ears; or the apple which he sees and smells is the same, but he sees in virtue of color and smells in virtue of odor : by reason of this we can say that the one seeing hears and the one hearing sees, and what is seen is smelled and what is smelled is seen. So, too, we can say that God is born of the Virgin because of His human nature, and this man is eternal because of the divine nature.

CHAPTER SEVEN

HOW THE ASSERTION: THE WORD OF GOD SUFFERED AND DIED, IS TO BE UNDERSTOOD, AND THAT NOTHING UNFITTING IS INVOLVED IN AFFIRMING THIS (23)

From the consideration, therefore, of the foregoing it can already be seen sufficiently that nothing inappropriate follows from the fact that we confess God, the only-begotten Word of God, to have suffered and died. For we do not ascribe these things to Him in virtue of His divine nature, but in virtue of His human nature which He assumed in the unity of His person for our salvation.

Should, however, someone object that God being omnipotent could have saved the human race in some way other than the death of His own, only-begotten Son, such an objector should reflect that in regard to the deeds of God one must consider precisely what can be done fittingly, even if God could have done this some other way : otherwise this type of reasoning would invalidate every one of His works. For when considering why God has designed heaven with a certain quantity and why He has established the stars in a certain number, it will occur to the wise thinker that these things could be accomplished fittingly thus, even if God could have done them otherwise. I affirm this, however, inasmuch as we believe the entire course of nature- including human acts- is subject to divine providence. For when the credibility of this is repudiated, all worship of the divinity is closed off. Hence, we undertake the present debate with those who claim to be worshipers of God whether they are Christians, or Muslims or Jews. With those, however, who say that everything comes from God by necessity, we have disputed elsewhere (24) at greater length.

If, therefore, anyone reflects piously on the fitting character of the Passion and Death of Christ, he will discover such a depth (25) of wisdom that something more and greater will always occur to the thinker, such that he will experience the truth of what the Apostle says: *"We preach Christ Crucified, unto the Jews indeed a stumbling block, and unto the Gentiles foolishness; but to us Christ the power of God and the wisdom of God."* (1 Cor. 1:23-24) And further (v. 25) : *"the foolishness of God is wiser than men."*

First, then, it comes to mind that, since Christ has assumed a human nature to repair the Fall of man, as we have already said above (See above, Chapter 5), it was necessary for Christ, according to His human nature to suffer and accomplish those things which could serve as a remedy for the fall into sin. Now, the sin of man consists principally in this : that being absorbed in corporeal goods he lost the spiritual. Therefore, it was quite fitting for the Son of God in His assumed nature to show men through the things He did and suffered that men should consider temporal goods or evils as nothing, lest impeded by an inordinate affection for them they might be less dedicated to spiritual things.

Hence, Christ chose poor parents, perfect nonetheless in virtue, lest anyone boast in mere nobility of the flesh or parental wealth. He led a poor life, that He might teach how to despise riches. He lived deprived of any social station, that He might recall men from an inordinate desire for honors. He endured work, hunger, thirst, whipping of His body, lest men intent on pleasures and delights be dissuaded from the good of virtue because of life's difficulties. Finally, He underwent death, lest for fear of death anyone desert the truth ; and lest anyone serving the truth fear death as shameful, He chose the most reproachful death possible (26), the death of the Cross. So, therefore, it was fitting for the Son of God made man to suffer death, that by His example He might stimulate men to virtue, that thus might be verified what Peter says, *"Christ has died for us leaving us an example that we might walk in His footsteps."* (1 Pet. 2:21)

Next, because for some men not only is right conduct whereby they avoid sins necessary to salvation, but also knowledge of the truth whereby they avoid errors, it was necessary for the restoration of the human race that the only-begotten Word of God assuming a human nature strengthen men in the certain knowledge of the truth.

An assent not entirely firm, however, is given a truth taught by man, because man can be deceived and deceive, but knowledge excluding any doubting of the truth is supported by God alone. So, then, it was necessary for the Son of God made man to propose to men the doctrine of divine truth, in such wise as to show it to be of divine, not human origin. And this indeed He shows by His many miracles. For one doing things which God alone can do, for instance, raising the dead, giving sight to the blind and by doing other suchlike, is to be believed in the things He says about God. For who works through God, is consequently someone who also speaks through God.

But those who were present could see His miracles ; by those coming later, however, they could only be believed to have been worked. Now, for this, Divine Wisdom provided a remedy in the weakness of Christ. For had He lived in the world rich, powerful and enjoying some great position, it could have been thought that His teaching and miracles were acknowledged out of human respect and by reason of His human power. And so to make it quite clear that this was a work of divine power, He chose the vilest and weakest in the world : a poor mother, a life of want, uneducated disciples and messengers, to be reproached and condemned finally to death by the rulers of the world, that it might clearly appear how the recognition of His miracles and teaching was not a matter of human, but of divine power.

Hence, in what He did and suffered there is conjoined human weakness and divine power : for at birth wrapped in swaddling clothes He is placed in a manger, but praised by the Angels and adored by Magi led by a star; He was tempted by the Devil but ministered to by Angels. He lived in want and as a beggar, but raises the dead, and gave sight to the blind; He died nailed to the gibbet, was numbered among thieves, but at His death the sun was darkened, the earth shaken, rocks rent, tombs opened and the bodies of the dead raised. Should anyone, therefore, from such beginnings see so great fruit attained, namely, the conversion of almost the entire world to Christ, and still seek other signs before believing, such a one may be adjudged harder than rock, since at His death even the rocks were rent (cf. Matt. 27: 51). This is why the Apostle writing to the Corinthians says : *"The word of the Cross, to them that persist, is foolishness, but to them that are saved, that is, to us, it is the power of God."* (1 Cor. 1: 18)

About this there is still another point to be considered, namely, that in accord with the same providential dispositions whereby in Himself the Son of God made man willed to suffer infirmity, He also willed His disciples, whom He appointed as ministers of human salvation, to be outcasts in the world. Hence, He did not choose the erudite and the noble, but the uneducated and lowly, namely poor fishermen. And sending them forth to seek the salvation of men He commanded them to observe poverty (cf. Luke 9: 3), to suffer persecutions (cf. Matt. 5: 10 and Mk: 9: 30) and ridicule and even undergo death (cf. Matt. 24: 9) for the truth, lest their preaching seem undertaken for the sake of some earthly advantage, and so that the salvation of the world could not be ascribed to human wisdom or power, but solely to divine power. Hence, neither in them, who appeared according to the world's standards as outcasts, was there any lack of divine power working marvels.

This was necessary, however, for human restoration,

that men learn not to trust proudly in themselves, but in God. The perfection of human justice requires that a man submit wholly to God, from whom he also hopes to gain every desirable good and recognizes each as attainable. His disciples, therefore, could in no way have been better formed to despise present worldly goods and bear till death any adversity than through the Passion and death of Christ. Hence, He also told them in John : *"If they have persecuted Me, they will persecute you, too."* (John 15: 20)

And, finally, it must be noticed how the order of justice has this characteristic that punishment is inflicted for sin. For it is apparent in human judgments that things done unjustly are reordered in accord with justice, when the judge takes from him, who accepting what is not his own has more than he should have, that more which he has and gives it to him who has less. Whoever sins, however, indulges his own will more than he ought; for to fulfill his own will he transgresses the order of reason and of the divine law. For this, then, that the will might be reduced to the order of justice, it is necessary that the will be withdrawn from that which it intends. This is effected when the person is punished either by deprivation of the goods which he wishes to have or by the infliction of evils which he is naturally disinclined to endure.

This reintegration of justice through punishment, therefore, sometimes is effected by the will of him who is punished, when he himself freely assumes the punishment, that he might return to justice; sometimes it is effected against his will, and in this case he, in fact, does not return to justice, but justice is fulfilled in him. Now, the entire human race was subject to sin. To be returned, therefore, to the state of justice required the interposition of some punishment which man would himself freely undertake to fulfill the order of divine justice.

There was, however, no mere man great enough to be able to satisfy God adequately by voluntarily assuming some punishment, even for his own sin, much less for the sin of the entire human race. For when man sins, he transgresses the law of God; and so to the extent that he is able injures God whose majesty is infinite. And the injury is so much the greater as the one against whom it is committed is greater. For it is obvious that the injury is considered greater if one strikes a soldier rather than a peasant, and still greater if one strikes a king or prince. Therefore, a sin committed against the law of God entails in some way an infinite injury.

But it must further be noticed that satisfaction is also measured in accord with the dignity of him who satisfies. For one word of apology by a king offered in satisfaction for some injury is considered greater than if anyone else should either kneel, or prostrate naked, or undertake any humiliation to satisfy someone injured. No mere man, however, had that infinite dignity such that his satisfaction could be reputed worthy in respect to the injury done God. Hence, it was necessary that some man of infinite dignity be found who would undergo punishment for all and so satisfy fully for the sins of the whole world. For this, then, the only-begotten Word of God, true God and Son of God, assumed a human nature and willed to suffer death in it, that satisfying He might cleanse the entire human race of sin. Hence, St. Peter also says, *"Christ died once for our sins, the Just for the unjust, that He might offer us to God."* (1 Pet. 3:18)

Therefore, it was not fitting, as Muslims opine, that God cleanse human sins without satisfaction, even less that He not permit man to fall into sin. For the first would be repugnant to the order of justice, the second to the order of human nature, whereby man is of his own will free, capable of choosing good or evil. It pertains to God's Providence, however, not to destroy, but to save the order of things. In this, then, the wisdom of God appears that He observes both the order of justice and of nature, and yet mercifully provides man a remedy of salvation through the Incarnation and death of His own Son.

CHAPTER EIGHT

HOW THE ASSERTION THAT THE FAITHFUL EAT THE BODY OF CHRIST IS TO BE UNDERSTOOD AND HOW NOTHING INAPPROPRIATE RESULTS FROM THIS (27)

Because, therefore, men are cleansed from sin through the Passion and death of Christ, and so that a lasting memory of this so immense blessing might remain in us, the Son of God, as the hour of His Passion approached, gave His own Body and Blood to the disciples under the species of bread and wine as the memorial of His Passion and death. To the very present day the Church of Christ continues to celebrate this memorial of His venerable Passion throughout the world.

How groundlessly the unbelievers mock this Sacrament anyone, even minimally instructed in the Christian religion, can easily perceive. For we do not claim that the Body of Christ is cut to pieces and thus divided is eaten by believers under the Sacrament, so that at some point the supply must fail, even if it have the magnitude of a mountain, as they say. But with the conversion of bread into the Body of Christ we assert the Body of Christ to be in a sacrament of the Church and to be eaten by the faithful. From the fact, therefore, that the Body of Christ is not divided, but something else is converted into it, it cannot follow at all that, when the faithful eat it, it be reduced in quantity.

Should the unbeliever, however, wish to say that this conversion is impossible, let him consider- if he confesses the omnipotence of God- that, since by natural power one thing can be changed as regards its form into another, as when air is changed into fire while the matter first subject to the form of air afterwards becomes subject to the form of fire; all the more the power of the omnipotent God, which produces the whole substance of a thing rather than merely transmuting at the level of form as nature does, can change this whole thing (28) into another whole thing, precisely as bread is changed into the Body of Christ and wine into His Blood.

If, however, someone should wish to object to this conversion on the basis of what the senses perceive, because nothing at the level of the senses is changed in the sacrament of the Altar, let such a one consider that all divine realities are so proposed to us that under the cover (29) of visible things they come to us. So, then, that the Body and Blood of Christ might be taken as a spiritual and divine repast and not as ordinary food and drink (30), they are eaten under the species of bread and wine, lest it be too horrifying to eat human flesh and drink human blood.

Nor, moreover, do we say that this comes to be as though those species in the sacrament of the Altar which appear to the senses exist solely in the imagination of the beholders, as happens with magical tricks, because no fiction is becoming to the Sacrament of truth. But God who is the Creator of substance and accident can conserve the sensible accidents in being, their subjects having been transmuted into something else. For He can by His own omnipotence both produce and conserve in being the effects of secondary causes without secondary causes. Should anyone not confess the omnipotence of God, however, we do not undertake to argue with him in the present work, but only against the Muslims and others who do confess the omnipotence of God.

Other mysteries of this Sacrament, however, are not to be discussed further here, because the mysteries of faith should not be displayed before unbelievers [infidelibus]. (31)

CHAPTER NINE

THAT THERE IS A SPECIAL PLACE WHERE SOULS ARE PURIFIED BEFORE RECEIVING BEATITUDE (32)

It remains now to consider the opinion of some who claim there is no purgatory after death. That some men should in fact have come to hold this position seems to have happened as happened with so many other errors. For some wishing to avoid certain errors, but lacking caution, fell into the contrary, as Arius who, while wishing to avoid Sabellius' error of confusing the persons of the Holy Trinity, fell into the opposite error of dividing the essence of the Godhead. Similarly, Eutyches, while he wished to avoid Nestorius' error (33) of dividing in Christ the person of God and of man, committed the contrary error of confessing one nature of God and of man. In such wise, then, others as well, while wishing to avoid Origen's error (34) of holding all punishment after death to be purgative (and none vindictive), fell into the opposite error of saying no punishment after death is purgative (but only vindictive).

Between these opposite errors, however, the holy Catholic and apostolic Church has carefully traced a middle position (35). For just as she distinguishes the persons in the Trinity against Sabellius, yet does not incline to the error of Arius, but confesses the essence of the three persons to be one; and just as in the mystery of the Incarnation on the other hand she distinguishes the natures against Eutyches, and does not divide the person with Nestorius : so also she confesses that in the state of souls after death some punishments are purgative, for those, namely, who leave this world without mortal sin in the state of charity and grace. Moreover, the Church does not with Origen confess all punishments to be purgative, but asserts those who die with mortal sin are afflicted by eternal torment together with the devil and his angels.

For the justification, therefore, of this assertion it seems necessary first to consider that those who die in mortal sin are immediately subjected to the torments of hell. This is clearly proven on gospel authority. For in Luke it is said by the mouth of the Lord that "*the rich man died*" at a banquet "*and was buried in hell*" (Lk. 16: 22) ; and the nature of his torment is evident from his own confession when he says: "*I am tormented in this flame*" (Ibid., 24). Through Job, too, it is said of the impious: "*They spend their days in wealth, and in a moment they do down to hell who have said to God: 'Depart from us, we desire not the knowledge of Thy ways'*" (Job 21: 13-14)."

Not only the impious, however, for their own sins, but also the just (36) before the suffering of Christ for the sin of our first parents, descended at death to hell [the underworld] . Hence Jacob said : "*I will go down to my son into Sheol, mourning.*" (Gen. 37 : 35) So, too, Christ Himself descended into hell, as stated in the Symbol of Faith [the Apostles' Creed], as beforehand it was predicted through the prophet : *"Thou wilt not leave my soul in hell"* (Ps. 15: 10), a passage referred to Christ by Peter in the Acts (Acts 2 : 27). Although Christ descended into hell in another manner, not as one guilty of sin, but among the dead as the only truly free man (37), He went down for the purpose of despoiling principalities and powers (cf. Col. 2: 15) and that He might lead captivity captive (Eph. 4 : 8). This was predicted beforehand through Zachary : *"Thou also by the blood of thy testament has sent forth thy prisoners out of the pit."* (Zach 9: 11)

But because the mercies of God are above all His works (cf. Ps. 144 : 9), it is all the more to be believed that those who die without stain immediately receive the wages of eternal compensation. And indeed this is plainly proved by clear texts. For the Apostle says in the second Letter to the Corinthians , after he has mentioned the tribulations of the saints: *"For we know"*, he says, *"if our earthly house of this habitation be dissolved, that we have a building of God, a house not made with hands, everlasting in heaven."* (2 Cor. 5: 1) From an initial study of these words it seems possible to conclude that on the dissolution of the mortal body man is clothed with heavenly glory. But that this interpretation might be clearer, let us discuss the following.

Precisely because he has proposed two points, namely, the dissolution of the earthly dwelling and the gaining of a heavenly home, he shows how the yearning of man is related to each, via a certain explanation of each. Hence, he first comments on the desire of a heavenly home, and says that *"We groan in this"*, impeded as it were by our desire " *to put on our heavenly dwelling"* (2 Cor. 5 : 2) Through this he also lets it be understood that that heavenly house which he says is above is not something separate from man, but something inhering in man. For man is not said to put on a house, but a garment, whereas one is said to dwell in a house. When, therefore, these two are linked as in the phrase *"clothed over with our heavenly dwelling",* he shows that the object desired is also something adhering because it is put on, and something containing and transcending because it is dwelt in. What that object desired is, however, will become clear from the following verses.

Because he did not simply say "clothed", but *"clothed over"*, he provides the explanation of his assertion adding : *"Provided that we be found clothed, and not naked"* (v. 3) , as though he had said : if the soul were so to be clothed with the heavenly habitation that it would not have to leave the earthly, the gaining of that heavenly dwelling would be a "clothing over". But because it is necessary to leave the earthly dwelling precisely to put on the heavenly, the clothing cannot be called a "clothing over", but only a simple clothing.

Now, someone could ask the Apostle : Why did you say *"desiring to be clothed over"*? To this he replies, adding (v. 4) : *"For we also, who are in this tabernacle"*, that is, who art clothed with our present transitory earthly tent, not having a permanent dwelling, *"do groan, being burdened"*, as it were, by some happening impeding our desire. By virtue of our natural desire *"we would not be stripped naked"* of our earthly tabernacle, but rather await being *"clothed upon"* with the heavenly tent so *"that which is mortal might be swallowed up by immortal life"*, that is, that we might pass to immortal life without tasting death.

Or again, someone might say to the Apostle : It seems reasonable that we should not want to be deprived of the earthly dwelling which is connatural to us ; but whence comes it that we yearn to be clothed with a heavenly dwelling? Replying to this, he answers : *"He who has prepared us for this very thing"* (v. 5), that we should desire the heavenly, *"is God"*. And how He does this in us he shows by adding : *"Who has given us the pledge of the Spirit."* For, through the Holy Spirit whom we receive from God we are made certain of the heavenly dwelling to be gained, as through a pledge enabling recovery from a debt : on the basis of this certainty, then, we are raised to the desire of a heavenly dwelling place.

Thus, there are two desires in us : one of nature not to leave our earthly dwelling, the other of grace to gain the heavenly dwelling. But these two desires cannot be fulfilled simultaneously, because we cannot arrive at the heavenly dwelling place, unless we leave the earthly. Hence, with a certain, firm confidence and daring we prefer the desire of grace to the desire of nature, such that we wish to leave the earthly dwelling and arrive at the heavenly. And this is what he means adding: *"Therefore having always confidence, knowing that, while we are in the body, we are absent from the Lord. For we walk by faith, and not by sight. But we are confident, and would rather be absent from the body, and at home with the Lord."* (vv. 6-8) Here it is evident that above he termed the corruptible body *"the earthly house of this habitation"* and *"tabernacle"*, for indeed the body is like a kind of garment to the soul.

So, too, the meaning of what he said above : *"a house not made by hands, everlasting in heaven"*, is made clear, because it is God Himself, whom men put on or dwell in while they are present with Him face to face, that is, seeing Him as He is; however, we are absent from Him while we hold by faith what we do not yet see. The saints, therefore, desire to be absent from the body, that is, so that their souls through death might be separated from the body, precisely that being thus absent from the body they might be present to the Lord. It is obvious, then, that the souls of the saints freed from their bodies arrive at a heavenly dwelling in seeing God. Therefore, the glory of saintly souls, which consists in the vision of God, is not postponed until the Day of Judgment when they resume their bodies.

This is also clear from the remark of the Apostle to the Philippians where he says : *"having a desire to be dissolved and to be with Christ"* (1 : 23) ; such a desire, however, would be unfulfilled, were Paul, who certainly is in heaven, not yet with Christ at the dissolution of his body. Plainly the Lord also said to the thief confessing on the cross : *"Today thou shalt be with Me in Paradise"* (Lk. 23 : 43), indicating by Paradise the enjoyment of glory. Hence, it is not to be believed that Christ in regard to the glory of their souls postpones the remuneration of His own faithful until the ressurection of the body. The assertion, therefore, which the Lord makes when He says : *"In My Father's house there are many mansions"* (John 14 : 2), has reference to the different rewards with which the saints in heavenly bliss are remunerated by God, not outside His heavenly home, but in the home itself.

Once, however, these points are grasped, it will consequently be seen there is a purgatory for souls after death. From many texts of Sacred Scripture it is obvious that no one with stain can reach that heavenly glory. In the book of Wisdom it is said of the sharing in divine wisdom that it is *"a certain pure emanation of the glory of Almighty God : and therefore no defiled thing comes into her."* (Wis. 7 : 25) Now, heavenly happiness consists in the perfect sharing of wisdom whereby we will see God face-to-face : therefore, it is necessary for them who are brought to that bliss to be absolutely without stain. The same is affirmed in Isaias :*"It shall be called the Holy Way : the unclean shall not pass over it."* (Is. 35 :8) And in the Apocalypse it is stated : *"There shall not enter into it anything defiled."* (Apoc. 21 : 27)

It happens, however, that some in the hour of death are defiled by some stains of sin, on account of which, nevertheless, they do not merit eternal damnation in hell, for instance venial sins such as idle words and other things of this kind. Therefore, those who die defiled by such faults cannot immediately on death enter heavenly glory. They could, however, as proven above, do so, were such stains not in them. At the least then, they endure a postponement of glory on account of venial sins. But there is no reason why our objectors should affirm that such souls after death should suffer more this punishment than any other, especially since for those consigned to hell the absence of the beatific vision and separation from God is a greater punishment than the torment of hell-fire suffered there. Therefore, the souls of those dying with venial sins suffer a cleansing fire after death.

Should anyone, however, claim that venial sins of this kind remain to be cleansed by the fire of conflagration (38) that will precede the face of the Judge at the end of the world, this is incompatible with the foregoing. For it has been shown above that the glory of the saints in whom there is no stain immediately at the dissolution of their body gain a heavenly dwelling ; nor can it be asserted that souls dying with venial sins can arrive at heavenly glory before they are cleansed of these, as has been shown above. For their glory, then, would be postponed to the Day of Judgment on account of venial sins. This seems absolutely improbable, namely, that for minor sins someone should suffer so great a punishment, i.e., the postponement of glory.

Further, it happens that some have been unable before death to complete the penance due for sins of which they have repented. Now it is not compatible with divine justice that they should not pay that penalty, for thus they who are suddenly overtaken by death would be in a better condition than those who have done daily penance for their sins in this life : therefore, they suffer after death punishment of this kind. Not, however, in hell, where men are punished for mortal sins, since their mortal sins have already been forgiven through penance ; nor would it be fitting for the payment of this penalty that the glory due them be postponed until the Day of Judgment. Hence, it is necessary to posit some temporal and cleansing punishment after this life before the Day of Judgment.

The ritual of the Church introduced by the Apostles (39) also harmonizes with this. For the whole Church prays (40) for the faithful departed. It is obvious, however, that she does not pray for those who are in hell, because in hell there is no redemption. Nor for those who have already gained eternal glory, because they have already reached the goal. It remains, therefore, that there exist certain temporal and cleansing penalties after this life, for whose remission the Church prays.

Hence, it is that the Apostle also says to the Corinthians : "*The fire shall try every man's work, of what sort it is. If any man's work abide, which he has built thereupon, he shall receive a reward. If any man's work burn, he shall suffer loss; but he himself shall be saved, yet so as by fire.*" (1 Cor. 3 :13-15) This, however, cannot be understood as meaning the fire of hell, because those who suffer this fire are not saved. Hence, it must be understood as referring to some purifying fire.

And indeed someone might say that this is to be understood of the fire which will precede the face of the Judge, especially because it is prefaced thus : "*For the Day of the Lord shall declare it, because it shall be revealed in fire.*" (v. 13) Now the Day of the Lord is understood to be the Day of his Final Coming, as the Apostle in *I Thessalonians* says

:"*The Day of the Lord shall so come, as a thief in the night.*" (I Thess. 5 : 2)

But it is to be noticed that, as the Day of Judgment is called the Day of the Lord because it is the day of His Coming for the universal judgment of the world, so the day of death of each is called the day of the Lord because in death Christ is said to come to each to reward or to condemn. Hence, in regard to the remuneration of good works He says to His disciples in John : "*And if I shall go, and prepare a place for you, I will come again, and will take you to Myself, that where I am, you also may be.*" (John 14 : 3) In regard, however, to condemnation of bad works it is said in the Apocalpse : "*Do penance, and do the first works. Or else I come to thee, and will move thy candlestand out of its place.*" (Apoc. 2: 5) The Day of the Lord, therefore, when He will come for the universal judgment will be revealed by fire which will precede the face of the Judge, by which the reprobate will be drawn into eternal torment, and by which the just who shall be found living will be cleansed. But the day of the Lord when He judges each at his death will be revealed in the fire which cleanses the good and condemns the wicked.

That there exists a purgatory after death, therefore, is made plain in this fashion.

CHAPTER TEN

THAT DIVINE PREDESTINATION PLACES NO
NECESSITY ON HUMAN ACTS AND HOW ONE
SHOULD PROCEED IN THIS QUESTION (41)

Now, finally, it remains to consider whether through divine preordering or predestination necessity is imposed on human acts. In this question caution advises one to proceed in such wise that truth be defended and any error or falsehood be avoided. For it would be erroneous to say that human acts and events are not subject to divine foreknowledge and ordering ; nor is it less erroneous to say that by reason of this divine foreknowledge and ordering necessity is imposed on human acts : for free will, the opportunity to consult, the utility of laws, care for doing good, and the justice of punishments and rewards would be destroyed. (42)

Therefore, one should recall that God has knowledge of things in a manner different from man. For man is subject to time, and so knows things in temporal fashion, contemplating some things as present, remembering other things as past, and foreseeing others as future. But God is above the course of time and His existence is eternal. Hence, His knowledge, too, is not temporal, but eternal.

Eternity, however, is compared to time (43) as something indivisible is compared to a continuum. For in time is found a certain diversity of parts succeeding each other according to before and after, as in a line are found diverse sections arranged according to their location to one another. But eternity has no before and after, because eternal things lack change. And so eternity is a simultaneous whole (44), as a point lacks parts distinguished by location.

A point, however, can be compared to a line on a twofold basis : in one way as included within a line, whether at the start of the line, or in the middle, or at the end ; in another way as existing outside the line. A point, therefore, existing within a line cannot be present to all the parts of the line, but in different parts of the line it is necessary to indicate diverse points. Nothing, however, prevents a point which is outside a line to be related equally to all parts of the line : as appears in a circle, whose center being indivisible in equally related to all parts of the circumference, and all of them are in some way present to it, although any one of them is not present to any other.

A moment, however, which is a limit of time, is likened to a point included in a line. It is not in fact present to all parts of time, but in different parts of time diverse moments are noted. Eternity, on the other hand, which being simple and indivisible embraces the entire course of time, in some way is likened to a point outside the line, namely to a center, and each part of time is equally present to it, although one part of time follows another.

God, then, who from the heights of eternity sees all things, thus knows as present the entire course of time and all which is accomplished in time. Therefore, when I see Socrates sitting, my knowledge is infallible and certain, but there is no necessity imposed on Socrates to be seated. Thus, God, viewing all things which to us are either past or present or future, knows all things infallibly and certainly, yet without imposing any necessity on contingent things.

Another example of this (45) can also be found if we compare the course of time to a journey. For, if anyone be on a road over which many travel, he indeed sees those who are just ahead of him; those, however, who come after him he cannot know with certainty. But if anyone be on some high elevation whence he can view the entire road, he sees all who pass by the way. Thus man who is in time cannot see simultaneously the entire course of time, but sees only those things which presently transpire before him, and a few things of the past, but he cannot know the future with certitude. God, however, from the heights of His eternity and with certainty sees as present all things which are done throughout the entire course of time, without in any way imposing any necessity on contingent things.

As, however, the divine knowledge does not impose necessity on contingent things, so neither does His disposing by which He providentially orders the universe. For He so orders things the way He acts on them. His ordering is not frustrated, for what He orders by His wisdom He executes by His power.

As regards the exercise of divine power, though, this must be considered, namely, that He works in all and moves each thing to its proper acts according to the mode proper to each ; such that some things by reason of the divine motion perform their actions necessarily, as is evident in the movements of heavenly bodies, others, however, contingently, and these sometimes fail in their proper activity, as is evident in the actions of corruptible bodies : a tree is sometimes impeded from producing fruit and an animal from begetting. Therefore, Divine Wisdom so orders things that the things so ordered occur according to the mode proper to each cause. The natural mode of man, however, is to act freely, not constrained by any necessity, because intelligent agents relate themselves to opposites ; so, then, God orders human acts, yet in such wise that human acts are not subjected to necessity, but stem from free will.

These, then, are the comments which here should be made upon the proposed questions, others being treated elsewhere (46) in greater detail.

ENDNOTES

1) Cf. Summa contra Gentiles IV, c. 91

2) According to Ricaldo de Monte Cruce, *Liber peregrinationis*, cap. 17 (ed. J.C.M. Laurent, Leipzig 1873), many of the Eastern dissidents held this opinion.

3) Possibly Syrian and Turkoman Muslims who accepted the Qur'an.

4) Cf. Qur'an, 95: "*He makes this one err, but that one believe*"; and LXXIV, 34: "*According to His good pleasure, He makes these to deviate thus and those to progress rightly*" (according to the translation of Robert Retenensis: ed. Theod. Bibliander 1550, pp. 90 and 179.

5) Cf. Summa contra Gentiles I, c. 2.

6) Ibid.

7) Cf. Summa contra Gentiles 1, c. 7 and 9; Summa Theologiae (ST) q. 32, a. 1.

8) Cf. Summa contra Gentiles IV, c. 11; Quaestiones Disputatae: De potentia Dei, Q. 2, a. 1 and q.10, a.1 and 2; S.T. I, q. 27 a.1 and 2; Expositio in Job ad litteram, cap. 1, lect. 1; Compendium theologiae., cap. 37-44.

9) Cf. Summa contra Gentiles IV, c. 19; Quaestiones Disputatae : De potentia Dei, q. 10 a. 1 and 2; S.T. I, q. 27, a. 3, Compendium theologiae, cap. 46-49.

10) Cf. Summa theologiae I-II, q. 28.

11) Cf. Summa theologiae I, q. 36 a. 2,

12) Cf. Quaestiones disputatae: De potentia Dei, q. 9 a. 1 and 2; Summa theologiae I, q. 29 a.2.

13) As noted in Chapters 3 and 4.

14) Cf. Scripta super libros Sententiarum, III d. 1q. 1 a. 2; Summa contra Gentiles IV c. 54 and 55; Summa theologiae III, q. 1 and 2; Compendium theologiae, cap. 200 and 201.

15) Cf. Summa contra Gentiles IV c. 39 and 41; Compendium theologiae, cap. 211.

16) Cf. St. Thomas, In decem libros Ethicorum expositio, IX 9 (1168 b 31)

17) Cf. Peter Lombard, Liber Sententiarum, 1 d. 37 and the texts of the Fathers cited there.

18) Cf. St. Thomas, In libros De anima expositio, III 7 (329 b 5) and De unitate Intellectus contra Averroistas, cap. 1.

19) Cf. above, paragraph 3 and ss.

20) Cf. Summa theologiae I, q. 29, a. 2.

21) Cf. above, paragraph 5.

22) Cf. Summa theologiae III, q. 16 a. 4 and 5.

23) Cf. St. Thomas, Scripta super libros Sententiarum, III d. 20 a. 1 qc. 3 and a. 4 qc. 2; Summa contra Gentiles IV c. 55; Quodl. II a. 2; Summa theologiae III, q. 40 a. 3, q. 46 a. 1-4, q. 50 a. 1; Compendium theologiae, cap. 227.

24) Cf. Summa contra Gentiles III c. 64, 72 and 73.

25) Cf. Summa contra Gentiles IV c. 54, at the beginning.

26) Cf. Augustine, *De diversis quaestionibus* 83, q. 25 (PL 34, 17), which St. Thomas cites in Summa theologiae III, q. 50 a. 1).

27) Cf. Summa contra Gentiles IV c. 53.

28) Cf. Summa theologiae III, q. 75 a. 4.

29) Cf. Isidore, *Libri Etymologiarum*, VI n. 19 n. 40 (PL 82, 255 C).

30) Cf. Summa contra Gentiles IV c. 61.

31) Cf. Decretum D. 43 c. 2 (ed. Friedberg I, 155) in

which, states John of Fano, *"It is said that the mysteries of our faith are not to be displayed before heretics and pagans."* (Corpus iuris cum Glossis, ed. Turin 1588, col. 239).

32) Cf. St.Thomas in "Scripta super libros Sententiarum, IV d. 21 q. 1 a. 1; Summa contra Gentiles IV c. 91; Compendium theologiae, cap. 181 and 182.

33) Cf. Summa contra Gentiles IV c. 35.

34) Cf. St. Augustine *De haeresibus* 43 (PL 42, 33) and *De civitate Dei* XXI, c. 17 (PL 41, 731).

35) Cf. Summa contra Gentiles IV c. 7, toward the end; Summa theologiae III, q. 2 a. 6.

36) Cf. St. Thomas, Scripta super libros Sententiarum, IV d. 45 q. 1, a. 2 qc. 1 and a. 3.

37) Cf. Peter Lombard, Liber Sententiarum, III d. 21 c. 1, paraphrasing Ps. 87, 6; cf. St. Augustine on Ps. 87 n. 5 (PL 36, 1111).

38) Cf. St. Thomas, Scripta super libros Sententiarum, IV d. 47 q. 2.

39) St. Thomas, Scripta super libros Sententiarum, IV d. 45 q. 2 a. 1 qc. 1, but c. 2 citing pseudo-John Damascene, *De iis qui in fide dormierunt n. 3* (PG 95, 249 B-C).

40) Cf. St. Augustine, *De cura pro mortuis gerenda,* N. 1 (PL 40, 592).

41) Cf. St. Thomas, Scripta super libros Sententiarum, 1 d. 28 a. 5; De Veritate, q. 2 a. 12; Quodlibet XI a. 3; Summa contra Gentiles III c. 72, 73 and 94; Summa theologiae I, q. 14 a. 13 and q. 22 a. 4; Super Metaph. VI 3; In libros Peri Hermeneias expositio, I 14; Compendium theologiae 133, 139 and 140.

42) Cf. Summa contra Gentiles III c. 73.

43) Cf. Summa contra Gentiles I c. 66.

44) Cf. Boethius, De consolatione Philosophiae, V prosa 6 (PL 63, 858 A).

45) Cf. St. Thomas, In libros Peri Hermeneias expositio, I 14 (Leon. n. 19)

46) St. Thomas refers to his work: the *Summa contra Gentiles.*

APPENDIX

ENCYCLICAL LETTER
AETERNI PATRIS

ON THE RESTORATION OF CHRISTIAN PHILOSOPHY
ACCORDING TO THE MIND OF
ST. THOMAS AQUINAS, THE ANGELIC DOCTOR

BY POPE LEO XIII

ENCYCLICAL LETTER
of
Pope Leo XIII

ON THE RESTORATION OF CHRISTIAN PHILOSOPHY ACCORDING TO THE MIND OF ST. THOMAS AQUINAS, THE ANGELIC DOCTOR

TO HIS VENERABLE BRETHREN, ALL THE PATRIARCHS, PRIMATES, ARCHBISHOPS, AND BISHOPS OF THE CATHOLIC WORLD, IN FAVOR AND COMMUNION WITH THE APOSTOLIC SEE.

VENERABLE BRETHREN,

HEALTH AND APOSTOLIC BENEDICTION.

The only-begotten Son of the Eternal Father, who came on earth to bring salvation and the light of divine wisdom to men, conferred a great and wonderful blessing on the world when, about to ascend again into heaven, He commanded the Apostles to go and teach all nations,[1] and left the Church which He had founded to be the common and supreme teacher of the peoples. For men whom the truth had set free were to be preserved by the truth; nor would the fruits of heavenly doctrines by which salvation comes to men have long remained had not the Lord Christ appointed an unfailing teaching authority to train the minds to faith. And the Church built upon the promises of its own divine Author, whose charity it imitated, so faithfully followed out His commands that its constant aim and chief wish was this: to teach religion and contend forever against errors. To this end assuredly have tended the incessant labors of individual bishops; to this end also the published laws and decrees of councils, and especially the constant watchfulness of the Roman Pontiffs, to whom, as successors of the blessed Peter in the primacy of the Apostles, belongs the right and office of teaching and confirming their brethren in the faith. Since, then, according to the warning of the apostle, the minds of Christ's faithful are apt to be deceived and the integrity of the faith to be corrupted among men by philosophy and vain deceit,[2] the supreme pastors of the Church have always thought it their duty to advance, by every means in their power, science truly so called, and at the same time to provide with special care that all studies should accord with the Catholic faith, especially philosophy, on which a right interpretation of the other sciences in great part depends. Indeed, venerable brethren, on this very subject among others, We briefly admonished you in Our first encyclical letter; but now, both by reason of the gravity of the subject and the condition of the time, we are again compelled to speak to you on the mode of taking up the study of philosophy which shall respond most fitly to the excellence of faith, and at the same time be consonant with the dignity of human science.

2. Whoso turns his attention to the bitter strifes of these days and seeks a reason for the troubles that vex public and private life must come to the conclusion that a fruitful cause of the evils which now afflict, as well as those which threaten, us lies in this: that false conclusions concerning divine and human things, which originated in the schools of philosophy, have now crept into all the orders of the State, and have been accepted by the common consent of the masses. For, since it is in the very nature of man to follow the guide of reason in his actions, if his intellect sins at all his will soon follows; and thus it happens that false opinions, whose seat is in the understanding, influence human actions and pervert them. Whereas, on the other hand, if men be of sound mind and take their stand on true and solid principles, there will result a vast amount of benefits for the public and private good. We do not, indeed, attribute such force and authority to philosophy as to esteem it equal to the task of combating and rooting out all errors; for, when the Christian religion was first constituted, it came upon earth to restore it to its primeval dignity by the admirable light of faith, diffused "not by persuasive words of human wisdom, but in the manifestation of spirit and of power",[3] so also at the present time we look above all things to the powerful help of Almighty God to bring back to a right understanding the minds of man and dispel the darkness of error.[4] But the natural helps with which the grace of the divine wisdom, strongly and sweetly disposing all things, has supplied the human race are neither to be despised nor neglected, chief among which is evidently the right use of

philosophy. For, not in vain did God set the light of reason in the human mind; and so far is the super-added light of faith from extinguishing or lessening the power of the intelligence that it completes it rather, and by adding to its strength renders it capable of greater things.

3. Therefore, Divine Providence itself requires that, in calling back the people to the paths of faith and salvation, advantage should be taken of human science also—an approved and wise practice which history testifies was observed by the most illustrious Fathers of the Church. They, indeed, were wont neither to belittle nor undervalue the part that reason had to play, as is summed up by the great Augustine when he attributes to this science "that by which the most wholesome faith is begotten . . . is nourished, defended, and made strong."[5]

4. In the first place, philosophy, if rightly made use of by the wise, in a certain way tends to smooth and fortify the road to true faith, and to prepare the souls of its disciples for the fit reception of revelation; for which reason it is well called by ancient writers sometimes a steppingstone to the Christian faith,[6] sometimes the prelude and help of Christianity,[7] sometimes the Gospel teacher.[8] And, assuredly, the God of all goodness, in all that pertains to divine things, has not only manifested by the light of faith those truths which human intelligence could not attain of itself, but others, also, not altogether unattainable by reason, that by the help of divine authority they may be made known to all at once and without any admixture of error. Hence it is that

certain truths which were either divinely proposed for belief, or were bound by the closest chains to the doctrine of faith, were discovered by pagan sages with nothing but their natural reason to guide them, were demonstrated and proved by becoming arguments. For, as the Apostle says, the invisible things of Him, from the creation of the world, are clearly seen, being understood by the things that are made: His eternal power also and divinity;[9] and the Gentiles who have not the Law show, nevertheless, the work of the Law written in their hearts.[10] But it is most fitting to turn these truths, which have been discovered by the pagan sages even, to the use and purposes of revealed doctrine, in order to show that both human wisdom and the very testimony of our adversaries serve to support the Christian faith—a method which is not of recent introduction, but of established use, and has often been adopted by the holy Fathers of the Church. What is more, those venerable men, the witnesses and guardians of religious traditions, recognize a certain form and figure of this in the action of the Hebrews, who, when about to depart out of Egypt, were commanded to take with them the gold and silver vessels and precious robes of the Egyptians, that by a change of use the things might be dedicated to the service of the true God which had formerly been the instruments of ignoble and superstitious rites. Gregory of Neo-Caesare[11] praises Origen expressly because, with singular dexterity, as one snatches weapons from the enemy, he turned to the defense of Christian wisdom and to the destruction of superstition many arguments drawn from the writings of the pagans. And both

Gregory of Nazianzen[12] and Gregory of Nyssa[13] praise and commend a like mode of disputation in Basil the Great; while Jerome[14] especially commends it in Quadratus, a disciple of the Apostles, in Aristides, Justin, Irenaeus, and very many others. Augustine says: "Do we not see Cyprian, that mildest of doctors and most blessed of martyrs, going out of Egypt laden with gold and silver and vestments? And Lactantius, also and Victorinus, Optatus and Hilary? And, not to speak of the living, how many Greeks have done likewise?"[15] But if natural reason first sowed this rich field of doctrine before it was rendered fruitful by the power of Christ, it must assuredly become more prolific after the grace of the Savior has renewed and added to the native faculties of the human mind. And who does not see that a plain and easy road is opened up to faith by such a method of philosophic study?

5. But the advantage to be derived from such a school of philosophy is not to be confined within these limits. The foolishness of those men who "by these good things that are seen could not understand Him, that is, neither by attending to the works could have acknowledged who was the workman,"[16] is gravely reproved in the words of Divine Wisdom. In the first place, then, this great and noble fruit is gathered from human reason, that it demonstrates that God is; for the greatness of the beauty and of the creature the Creator of them may be seen so as to be known thereby.[17] Again, it shows God to excel in the height of all perfections, especially in infinite wisdom before which nothing lies hidden, and in absolute justice which no de-

praved affection could possibly shake; and that God, therefore, is not only true but truth itself, which can neither deceive nor be deceived. Whence it clearly follows that human reason finds the fullest faith and authority united in the word of God. In like manner, reason declares that the doctrine of the Gospel has even from its very beginning been made manifest by certain wonderful signs, the established proofs, as it were, of unshaken truth; and that all, therefore, who set faith in the Gospel do not believe rashly as though following cunningly devised fables,[18] but, by a most reasonable consent, subject their intelligence and judgment to an authority which is divine. And of no less importance is it that reason most clearly sets forth that the Church instituted by Christ (as laid down in the Vatican Council), on account of its wonderful spread, its marvelous sanctity, and its incxhaustible fecundity in all places, as well as of its Catholic unity and unshaken stability, is in itself a great and perpetual motive of belief and an irrefragable testimony of its own divine mission.[19]

6. Its solid foundations having been thus laid, a perpetual and varied service is further required of philosophy, in order that sacred theology may receive and assume the nature, form, and genius of a true science. For in this, the most noble of studies, it is of the greatest necessity to bind together, as it were, in one body the many and various parts of the heavenly doctrines, that, each being allotted to its own proper place and derived from its own proper principles, the whole may join together in a complete union; in

order, in fine, that all and each part may be strengthened by its own and the others' invincible arguments. Nor is that more accurate or fuller knowledge of the things that are believed, and somewhat more lucid understanding, as far as it can go, of the very mysteries of faith which Augustine and the other fathers commended and strove to reach, and which the Vatican Council itself[20] declared to be most fruitful, to be passed over in silence or belittled. Those will certainly more fully and more easily attain that knowledge and understanding who to integrity of life and love of faith join a mind rounded and finished by philosophic studies, as the same Vatican Council teaches that the knowledge of such sacred dogmas ought to be sought as well from analogy of the things that are naturally known as from the connection of those mysteries one with another and with the final end of man.[21]

7. Lastly, the duty of religiously defending the truths divinely delivered, and of resisting those who dare oppose them, pertains to philosophic pursuits. Wherefore, it is the glory of philosophy to be esteemed as the bulwark of faith and the strong defense of religion. As Clement of Alexandria testifies, the doctrine of the Savior is indeed perfect in itself and wanteth naught, since it is the power and wisdom of God. And the assistance of the Greek philosophy maketh not the truth more powerful; but, inasmuch as it weakens the contrary arguments of the sophists and repels the veiled attacks against the truth, it has been fitly called the hedge and fence of the vine.[22] For, as the enemies of the Catholic name, when about to attack religion, are in the habit of

borrowing their weapons from the arguments of philosophers, so the defenders of sacred science draw many arguments from the store of philosophy which may serve to uphold revealed dogmas. Nor is the triumph of the Christian faith a small one in using human reason to repel powerfully and speedily the attacks of its adversaries by the hostile arms which human reason itself supplied. This species of religious strife St. Jerome, writing to Magnus, notices as having been adopted by the Apostle of the Gentiles himself; Paul, the leader of the Christian army and the invincible orator, battling for the cause of Christ, skillfully turns even a chance inscription into an argument for the faith; for he had learned from the true David to wrest the sword from the hands of the enemy and to cut off the head of the boastful Goliath with his own weapon.[23] Moreover, the Church herself not only urges, but even commands, Christian teachers to seek help from philosophy. For, the fifth Lateran Council, after it had decided that "every assertion contrary to the truth of revealed faith is altogether false, for the reason that it contradicts, however slightly, the truth,"[24] advises teachers of philosophy to pay close attention to the exposition of fallacious arguments; since, as Augustine testifies, "if reason is turned against the authority of sacred Scripture, no matter how specious it may seem, it errs in the likeness of truth; for true it cannot be."[25]

8. But in order that philosophy may be bound equal to the gathering of those precious fruits which we have indicated, it behooves it above all things never to turn aside from that path which the Fathers have entered upon from a

venerable antiquity, and which the Vatican Council solemnly and authoritatively approved. As it is evident that very many truths of the supernatural order which are far beyond the reach of the keenest intellect must be accepted, human reason, conscious of its own infirmity, dare not affect to itself too great powers, nor deny those truths, nor measure them by its own standard, nor interpret them at will; but receive them, rather, with a full and humble faith, and esteem it the highest honor to be allowed to wait upon heavenly doctrines like a handmaid and attendant, and by God's goodness attain to them in any way whatsoever. But in the case of such doctrines as the human intelligence may perceive, it is equally just that philosophy should make use of its own method, principles, and arguments—not, indeed, in such fashion as to seem rashly to withdraw from the divine authority. But, since it is established that those things which become known by revelation have the force of certain truth, and that those things which war against faith war equally against right reason, the Catholic philosopher will know that he violates at once faith and the laws of reason if he accepts any conclusion which he understands to be opposed to revealed doctrine.

9. We know that there are some who, in their overestimate of the human faculties, maintain that as soon as man's intellect becomes subject to divine authority it falls from its native dignity, and hampered by the yoke of this species of slavery, is much retarded and hindered in its progress toward the supreme truth and excellence. Such an idea is most

false and deceptive, and its sole tendency is to induce foolish and ungrateful men willfully to repudiate the most sublime truths, and reject the divine gift of faith, from which the fountains of all good things flow out upon civil society. For the human mind, being confined within certain limits, and those narrow enough, is exposed to many errors and is ignorant of many things; whereas the Christian faith, reposing on the authority of God, is the unfailing mistress of truth, whom whoso followeth he will be neither enmeshed in the snares of error nor tossed hither and thither on the waves of fluctuating opinion. Those, therefore, who to the study of philosophy unite obedience to the Christian faith, are philosophizing in the best possible way; for the splendor of the divine truths, received into the mind, helps the understanding, and not only detracts in nowise from its dignity, but adds greatly to its nobility, keenness, and stability. For surely that is a worthy and most useful exercise of reason when men give their minds to disproving those things which are repugnant to faith and proving the things which conform to faith. In the first case they cut the ground from under the feet of error and expose the viciousness of the arguments on which error rests; while in the second case they make themselves masters of weighty reasons for the sound demonstration of truth and the satisfactory instruction of any reasonable person. Whoever denies that such study and practice tend to add to the resources and expand the faculties of the mind must necessarily and absurdly hold that the mind gains nothing from discriminating between the true and the false. Justly, therefore, does the Vatican

Council commemorate in these words the great benefits which faith has conferred upon reason: Faith frees and saves reason from error, and endows it with manifold knowledge.[26] A wise man, therefore, would not accuse faith and look upon it as opposed to reason and natural truths, but would rather offer heartfelt thanks to God, and sincerely rejoice that, in the density of ignorance and in the flood-tide of error, holy faith, like a friendly star, shines down upon his path and points out to him the fair gate of truth beyond all danger of wandering.

10. If, venerable brethren, you open the history of philosophy, you will find all We have just said proved by experience. The philosophers of old who lacked the gift of faith, yet were esteemed so wise, fell into many appalling errors. You know how often among some truths they taught false and incongruous things; what vague and doubtful opinions they held concerning the nature of the Divinity, the first origin of things, the government of the world, the divine knowledge of the future, the cause and principle of evil, the ultimate end of man, the eternal beatitude, concerning virtue and vice, and other matters, a true and certain knowledge of which is most necessary to the human race; while, on the other hand, the early Fathers and Doctors of the Church, who well understood that, according to the divine plan, the restorer of human science is Christ, who is the power and the wisdom of God,[27] and in whom are hid all the treasures of wisdom and knowledge,[28] took up and investigated the books of the ancient philosophers, and compared their teachings with the doctrines of revelation, and,

carefully sifting them, they cherished what was true and wise in them and amended or rejected all else. For, as the all-seeing God against the cruelty of tyrants raised up mighty martyrs to the defense of the Church, men prodigal of their great lives, in like manner to false philosophers and heretics He opposed men of great wisdom, to defend, even by the aid of human reason, the treasure of revealed truths. Thus, from the very first ages of the Church, the Catholic doctrine has encountered a multitude of most bitter adversaries, who, deriding the Christian dogmas and institutions, maintained that there were many gods, that the material world never had a beginning or cause, and that the course of events was one of blind and fatal necessity, not regulated by the will of Divine Providence.

11. But the learned men whom We call apologists speedily encountered these teachers of foolish doctrine and, under the guidance of faith, found arguments in human wisdom also to prove that one God, who stands pre-eminent in every kind of perfection, is to be worshipped; that all things were created from nothing by His omnipotent power; that by His wisdom they flourish and serve each their own special purposes. Among these St. Justin Martyr claims the chief place. After having tried the most celebrated academies of the Greeks, he saw clearly, as he himself confesses, that he could only draw truths in their fullness from the doctrine of revelation. These he embraced with all the ardor of his soul, purged of calumny, courageously and fully defended before the Roman emperors, and reconciled with them not a few of the sayings of the Greek philosophers.

12. Quadratus, also, and Aristides, Hermias, and Athenagoras stood nobly forth in that time. Nor did Irenaeus, the invincible martyr and Bishop of Lyons, win less glory in the same cause when, forcibly refuting the perverse opinions of the Orientals, the work of the Gnostics, scattered broadcast over the territories of the Roman Empire, he explained (according to Jerome) the origin of each heresy and in what philosophic source it took its rise.[29] But who knows not the disputations of Clement of Alexandria, which the same Jerome thus honorably commemorates: "What is there in them that is not learned, and what that is not of the very heart of philosophy?"[30] He himself, indeed, with marvelous versatility treated of many things of the greatest utility for preparing a history of philosophy, for the exercise of the dialectic art, and for showing the agreement between reason and faith. After him came Origen, who graced the chair of the school of Alexandria, and was most learned in the teachings of the Greeks and Orientals. He published many volumes, involving great labor, which were wonderfully adapted to explain the divine writings and illustrate the sacred dogmas; which, though, as they now stand, not altogether free from error, contain nevertheless a wealth of knowledge tending to the growth and advance of natural truths. Tertullian opposes heretics with the authority of the sacred writings; with the philosophers he changes his fence and disputes philosophically; but so learnedly and accurately did he confute them that he made bold to say: "Neither in science nor in schooling are we equals, as you imagine."[31] Arnobius, also, in his works against the pagans, and

Lactantius in the divine Institutions especially, with equal eloquence and strength strenuously strive to move men to accept the dogmas and precepts of Catholic wisdom, not by philosophic juggling, after the fashion of the Academicians, but vanquishing them partly by their own arms, and partly by arguments drawn from the mutual contentions of the philosophers.[32] But the writings on the human soul, the divine attributes, and other questions of mighty moment which the great Athanasius and Chrysostom, the prince of orators, have left behind them are, by common consent, so supremely excellent that it seems scarcely anything could be added to their subtlety and fullness. And, not to cover too wide a range, we add to the number of the great men of whom mention has been made the names of Basil the Great and of the two Gregories, who, on going forth from Athens, that home of all learning, thoroughly equipped with all the harness of philosophy, turned the wealth of knowledge which each had gathered up in a course of zealous study to the work of refuting heretics and preparing Christians.

13. But Augustine would seem to have wrested the palm from all. Of a most powerful genius and thoroughly saturated with sacred and profane learning, with the loftiest faith and with equal knowledge, he combated most vigorously all the errors of his age. What topic of philosophy did he not investigate? What region of it did he not diligently explore, either in expounding the loftiest mysteries of the faith to the faithful, or defending them against the full onslaught of adversaries, or again when, in demolishing the fables of the Academicians or the Manichaeans, he laid the safe founda-

tions and sure structure of human science, or followed up the reason, origin, and causes of the evils that afflict man? How subtly he reasoned on the angels, the soul, the human mind, the will and free choice, on religion and the life of the blessed, on time and eternity, and even on the very nature of changeable bodies. Afterwards, in the East, John Damascene, treading in the footsteps of Basil and of Gregory of Nazianzen, and in the West, Boethius and Anselm following the doctrines of Augustine, added largely to the patrimony of philosophy.

14. Later on, the doctors of the middle ages, who are called Scholastics, addressed themselves to a great work—that of diligently collecting, and sifting, and storing up, as it were, in one place, for the use and convenience of posterity the rich and fertile harvests of Christian learning scattered abroad in the voluminous works of the holy Fathers. And with regard, venerable brethren, to the origin, drift, and excellence of this scholastic learning, it may be well here to speak more fully in the words of one of the wisest of Our predecessors, Sixtus V: "By the divine favor of Him who alone gives the spirit of science, and wisdom, and understanding, and who though all ages, as there may be need, enriches His Church with new blessings and strengthens it with new safeguards, there was founded by Our fathers, men of eminent wisdom, the scholastic theology, which two glorious doctors in particular, the angelic St. Thomas and the seraphic St. Bonaventure, illustrious teachers of this faculty, . . . with surpassing genius, by unwearied diligence, and at the cost of long labors and vigils, set in order and

beautified, and when skillfully arranged and clearly explained in a variety of ways, handed down to posterity.

15. "And, indeed, the knowledge and use of so salutary a science, which flows from the fertilizing founts of the sacred writings, the sovereign Pontiffs, the holy Fathers and the councils, must always be of the greatest assistance to the Church, whether with the view of really and soundly understanding and interpreting the Scriptures, or more safely and to better purpose reading and explaining the Fathers, or for exposing and refuting the various errors and heresies; and in these late days, when those dangerous times described by the Apostle are already upon us, when the blasphemers, the proud, and the seducers go from bad to worse, erring themselves and causing others to err, there is surely a very great need of confirming the dogmas of Catholic faith and confuting heresies."

16. Although these words seem to bear reference solely to Scholastic theology, nevertheless they may plainly be accepted as equally true of philosophy and its praises. For, the noble endowments which make the Scholastic theology so formidable to the enemies of truth—to wit, as the same Pontiff adds, "that ready and close coherence of cause and effect, that order and array as of a disciplined army in battle, those clear definitions and distinctions, that strength of argument and those keen discussions, by which light is distinguished from darkness, the true from the false, expose and strip naked, as it were, the falsehoods of heretics wrapped around by a cloud of subterfuges and fallacies"[33]—those

noble and admirable endowments, We say, are only to be found in a right use of that philosophy which the Scholastic teachers have been accustomed carefully and prudently to make use of even in theological disputations. Moreover, since it is the proper and special office of the Scholastic theologians to bind together by the fastest chain human and divine science, surely the theology in which they excelled would not have gained such honor and commendation among men if they had made use of a lame and imperfect or vain philosophy.

17. Among the Scholastic Doctors, the chief and master of all towers Thomas Aquinas, who, as Cajetan observes, because "he most venerated the ancient Doctors of the Church, in a certain way seems to have inherited the intellect of all."[34] The doctrines of those illustrious men, like the scattered members of a body, Thomas collected together and cemented, distributed in wonderful order, and so increased with important additions that he is rightly and deservedly esteemed the special bulwark and glory of the Catholic faith. With his spirit at once humble and swift, his memory ready and tenacious, his life spotless throughout, a lover of truth for its own sake, richly endowed with human and divine science, like the sun he heated the world with the warmth of his virtues and filled it with the splendor of his teaching. Philosophy has no part which he did not touch finely at once and thoroughly; on the laws of reasoning, on God and incorporeal substances, on man and other sensible things, on human actions and their principles, he reasoned in such a manner that in him there is wanting neither a full

array of questions, nor an apt disposal of the various parts, nor the best method of proceeding, nor soundness of principles or strength of argument, nor clearness and elegance of style, nor a facility for explaining what is abstruse.

18. Moreover, the Angelic Doctor pushed his philosophic inquiry into the reasons and principles of things, which because they are most comprehensive and contain in their bosom, so to say, the seeds of almost infinite truths, were to be unfolded in good time by later masters and with a goodly yield. And as he also used this philosophic method in the refutation of error, he won this title to distinction for himself: that, single-handed, he victoriously combated the errors of former times, and supplied invincible arms to put those to rout which might in after-times spring up. Again, clearly distinguishing, as is fitting, reason from faith, while happily associating the one with the other, he both preserved the rights and had regard for the dignity of each; so much so, indeed, that reason. borne on the wings of Thomas to its human height, can scarcely rise higher, while faith could scarcely expect more or stronger aids from reason than those which she has already obtained through Thomas.

19. For these reasons most learned men, in former ages especially, of the highest repute in theology and philosophy, after mastering with infinite pains the immortal works of Thomas, gave themselves up not so much to be instructed in his angelic wisdom as to be nourished upon it. It is known that nearly all the founders and lawgivers of the religious orders commanded their members to study and religiously

adhere to the teachings of St. Thomas, fearful least any of them should swerve even in the slightest degree from the footsteps of so great a man. To say nothing of the family of St. Dominic, which rightly claims this great teacher for its own glory, the statutes of the Benedictines, the Carmelites, the Augustinians, the Society of Jesus, and many others all testify that they are bound by this law.

20. And, here, how pleasantly one's thoughts fly back to those celebrated schools and universities which flourished of old in Europe—to Paris, Salamanca, Alcala, to Douay, Toulouse, and Louvain, to Padua and Bologna, to Naples and Coimbra, and to many another! All know how the fame of these seats of learning grew with their years, and that their judgment, often asked in matters of grave moment, held great weight everywhere. And we know how in those great homes of human wisdom, as in his own kingdom, Thomas reigned supreme; and that the minds of all, of teachers as well as of taught, rested in wonderful harmony under the shield and authority of the Angelic Doctor.

21. But, furthermore, Our predecessors in the Roman pontificate have celebrated the wisdom of Thomas Aquinas by exceptional tributes of praise and the most ample testimonials. Clement VI in the bull "In Ordine;" Nicholas V in his brief to the friars of the Order of Preachers, 1451; Benedict XIII in the bull "Pretiosus," and others bear witness that the universal Church borrows luster from his admirable teaching; while St. Pius V declares in the bull "Mirabilis" that heresies, confounded and convicted by the

same teaching, were dissipated, and the whole world daily freed from fatal errors; others, such as Clement XII in the bull "Verbo Dei," affirm that most fruitful blessings have spread abroad from his writings over the whole Church, and that he is worthy of the honor which is bestowed on the greatest Doctors of the Church, on Gregory and Ambrose, Augustine and Jerome; while others have not hesitated to propose St. Thomas for the exemplar and master of the universities and great centers of learning whom they may follow with unfaltering feet. On which point the words of Blessed Urban V to the University of Toulouse are worthy of recall: "It is our will, which We hereby enjoin upon you, that ye follow the teaching of Blessed Thomas as the true and Catholic doctrine and that ye labor with all your force to profit by the same."[35] Innocent XII, followed the example of Urban in the case of the University of Louvain, in the letter in the form of a brief addressed to that university on February 6, 1694, and Benedict XIV in the letter in the form of a brief addressed on August 26, 1752, to the Dionysian College in Granada; while to these judgments of great Pontiffs on Thomas Aquinas comes the crowning testimony of Innocent VI: "His teaching above that of others, the canonical writings alone excepted, enjoys such a precision of language, an order of matters, a truth of conclusions, that those who hold to it are never found swerving from the path of truth, and he who dare assail it will always be suspected of error."[36]

22. The ecumenical councils, also, where blossoms the flower of all earthly wisdom, have always been careful to

hold Thomas Aquinas in singular honor. In the Councils of Lyons, Vienna, Florence, and the Vatican one might almost say that Thomas took part and presided over the deliberations and decrees of the Fathers, contending against the errors of the Greeks, of heretics and rationalists, with invincible force and with the happiest results. But the chief and special glory of Thomas, one which he has shared with none of the Catholic Doctors, is that the Fathers of Trent made it part of the order of conclave to lay upon the altar, together with sacred Scripture and the decrees of the supreme Pontiffs, the "Summa" of Thomas Aquinas, whence to seek counsel, reason, and inspiration.

23. A last triumph was reserved for this incomparable man—namely, to compel the homage, praise, and admiration of even the very enemies of the Catholic name. For it has come to light that there were not lacking among the leaders of heretical sects some who openly declared that, if the teaching of Thomas Aquinas were only taken away, they could easily battle with all Catholic teachers, gain the victory, and abolish the Church.[37] A vain hope, indeed, but no vain testimony.

24. Therefore, venerable brethren, as often as We contemplate the good, the force, and the singular advantages to be derived from his philosophic discipline which Our Fathers so dearly loved. We think it hazardous that its special honor should not always and everywhere remain, especially when it is established that daily experience, and the judgment of the greatest men, and, to crown all, the voice of the Church, have favored the Scholastic philosophy. Moreover,

to the old teaching a novel system of philosophy has succeeded here and there, in which We fail to perceive those desirable and wholesome fruits which the Church and civil society itself would prefer. For it pleased the struggling innovators of the sixteenth century to philosophize without any respect for faith, the power of inventing in accordance with his own pleasure and bent being asked and given in turn by each one. Hence, it was natural that systems of philosophy multiplied beyond measure, and conclusions differing and clashing one with another arose about those matters even which are the most important in human knowledge. From a mass of conclusions men often come to wavering and doubt; and who knows not how easily the mind slips from doubt to error? But, as men are apt to follow the lead given them, this new pursuit seems to have caught the souls of certain Catholic philosophers, who, throwing aside the patrimony of ancient wisdom, chose rather to build up a new edifice than to strengthen and complete the old by aid of the new—ill-advisedly, in sooth, and not without detriment to the sciences. For, a multiform system of this kind, which depends on the authority and choice of any professor, has a foundation open to change, and consequently gives us a philosophy not firm, and stable, and robust like that of old, but tottering and feeble. And if, perchance, it sometimes finds itself scarcely equal to sustain the shock of its foes, it should recognize that the cause and the blame lie in itself. In saying this We have no intention of discountenancing the learned and able men who bring their industry and erudition, and, what is more, the wealth of new discoveries, to the service of philosophy; for, of course, We understand that this tends to the development of learning. But one should be very careful lest all or his chief labor be exhausted in these pursuits and in mere erudition. And the same thing is true of sacred theology, which, indeed, may be assisted and illustrated by all kinds of erudition, though it is absolutely necessary to approach it in the grave manner of the Scholastics, in order that, the forces of revelation and reason being united in it, it may continue to be "the invincible bulwark of the faith."[38]

25. With wise forethought, therefore,.not a few of the advocates of philosophic studies, when turning their minds recently to the practical reform of philosophy, aimed and aim at restoring the renowned teaching of Thomas Aquinas and winning it back to its ancient beauty.

26. We have learned with great joy that many members of your order, venerable brethren, have taken this plan to heart; and while We earnestly commend their efforts, We exhort them to hold fast to their purpose, and remind each and all of you that Our first and most cherished idea is that you should all furnish to studious youth a generous and copious supply of those purest streams of wisdom flowing inexhaustibly from the precious fountainhead of the Angelic Doctor.

27. Many are the reasons why We are so desirous of this. In the first place, then, since in the tempest that is on us the Christian faith is king constantly assailed by the machinations and craft of a certain false wisdom, all youths, but

especially those who are the growing hope of the Church, should be nourished on the strong and robust food of doctrine, that so, mighty in strength and armed at all points, they may become habituated to advance the cause of religion with force and judgment, "being ready always, according to the apostolic counsel, to satisfy every one that asketh you a reason of that hope which is in you,"[39] and that they may be able to exhort in sound doctrine and to convince the gainsayers.[40] Many of those who, with minds alienated from the faith, hate Catholic institutions, claim reason as their sole mistress and guide. Now, We think that, apart from the supernatural help of God, nothing is better calculated to heal those minds and to bring them into favor with the Catholic faith than the solid doctrine of the Fathers and the Scholastics, who so clearly and forcibly demonstrate the firm foundations of the faith, its divine origin, its certain truth, the arguments that sustain it. the benefits it has conferred on the human race, and its perfect accord with reason, in a manner to satisfy completely minds open to persuasion, however unwilling and repugnant.

28. Domestic and civil society even, which, as all see, is exposed to great danger from this plague of perverse opinions, would certainly enjoy a far more peaceful and secure existence if a more wholesome doctrine were taught in the universities and high schools—one more in conformity with the teaching of the Church, such as is contained in the works of Thomas Aquinas.

29. For, the teachings of Thomas on the true meaning of liberty, which at this time is running into license, on the

divine origin of all authority, on laws and their force, on the paternal and just rule of princes, on obedience to the higher powers, on mutual charity one toward another—on all of these and kindred subjects—have very great and invincible force to overturn those principles of the new order which are well known to be dangerous to the peaceful order of things and to public safety. In short, all studies ought to find hope of advancement and promise of assistance in this restoration of philosophic discipline which We have proposed. The arts were wont to draw from philosophy, as from a wise mistress, sound judgment and right method, and from it, also, their spirit, as from the common fount of life. When philosophy stood stainless in honor and wise in judgment, then, as facts and constant experience showed, the liberal arts flourished as never before or since; but, neglected and almost blotted out, they lay prone, since philosophy began to lean to error and join hands with folly. Nor will the physical sciences themselves, which are now in such great repute, and by the renown of so many inventions draw such universal admiration to themselves, suffer detriment, but find very great assistance in the restoration of the ancient philosophy. For, the investigation of facts and the contemplation of nature is not alone sufficient for their profitable exercise and advance; but, when facts have been established, it is necessary to rise and apply ourselves to the study of the nature of corporeal things, to inquire into the laws which govern them and the principles whence their order and varied unity and mutual attraction in diversity arise. To such investigations it is wonderful what force and light and aid the Scholastic philosophy, if judiciously taught would bring.

30. And here it is well to note that our philosophy can only by the grossest injustice be accused of being opposed to the advance and development of natural science. For, when the Scholastics, following the opinion of the holy Fathers, always held in anthropology that the human intelligence is only led to the knowledge of things without body and matter by things sensible, they well understood that nothing was of greater use to the philosopher than diligently to search into the mysteries of nature and to be earnest and constant in the study of physical things. And this they confirmed by their own example; for St. Thomas, Blessed Albertus Magnus, and other leaders of the Scholastics were never so wholly rapt in the study of philosophy as not to give large attention to the knowledge of natural things; and, indeed, the number of their sayings and writings on these subjects, which recent professors approve of and admit to harmonize with truth, is by no means small. Moreover, in this very age many illustrious professors of the physical sciences openly testify that between certain and accepted conclusions of modern physics and the philosophic principles of the schools there is no conflict worthy of the name.

31. While, therefore, We hold that every word of wisdom, every useful thing by whomsoever discovered or planned, ought to be received with a willing and grateful mind, We exhort you, venerable brethren, in all earnestness to restore the golden wisdom of St. Thomas, and to spread it far and wide for the defense and beauty of the Catholic

faith, for the good of society, and for the advantage of all the sciences. The wisdom of St. Thomas, We say; for if anything is taken up with too great subtlety by the Scholastic doctors, or too carelessly stated—if there be anything that ill agrees with the discoveries of a later age, or, in a word, improbable in whatever way—it does not enter Our mind to propose that for imitation to Our age. Let carefully selected teachers endeavor to implant the doctrine of Thomas Aquinas in the minds of students, and set forth clearly his solidity and excellence over others. Let the universities already founded or to be founded by you illustrate and defend this doctrine, and use it for the refutation of prevailing errors. But, lest the false for the true or the corrupt for the pure be drunk in, be ye watchful that the doctrine of Thomas be drawn from his own fountains, or at least from those rivulets which, derived from the very fount, have thus far flowed, according to the established agreement of learned men, pure and clear; be careful to guard the minds of youth from those which are said to flow thence, but in reality are gathered from strange and unwholesome streams.

32. But well do We know that vain will be Our efforts unless, venerable brethren, He helps Our common cause who, in the words of divine Scripture, is called the God of all knowledge;[41] by which we are also admonished that "every best gift and every perfect gift is from above, coming down from the Father of lights",[42] and again: "If any of you want wisdom, let him ask of God, who giveth to all men abundantly, and upbraideth not: and it shall be given him."[43]

33. Therefore in this also let us follow the example of the Angelic Doctor, who never gave himself to reading or writing without first begging the blessing of God, who modestly confessed that whatever he knew he had acquired not so much by his own study and labor as by the divine gift; and therefore let us all, in humble and united prayer, beseech God to send forth the spirit of knowledge and of understanding to the children of the Church and open their senses for the understanding of wisdom. And that we may receive fuller fruits of the divine goodness, offer up to God the most efficacious patronage of the Blessed Virgin Mary, who is called the seat of wisdom; having at the same time as advocates St. Joseph, the most chaste spouse of the Virgin, and Peter and Paul, the chiefs of the Apostles, whose truth renewed the earth which had fallen under the impure blight of error, filling it with the light of heavenly wisdom.

34. In fine, relying on the divine assistance and confiding in your pastoral zeal, most lovingly We bestow on all of you, venerable brethren, on all the clergy and the flocks committed to your charge, the apostolic benediction as a pledge of heavenly gifts and a token of Our special esteem.Given at St. Peter's, in Rome, the fourth day of August, 1879, the second year of our pontificate

.

⤞ ENDNOTES TO APPENDIX ⤝

1. Matt. 28: 19.

2. Col. 2:8.

3. I Cor. 2:4.

4. See "Inscrutabili Dei consilio," 78:113.

5. "De Trinitate," 14, 1, 3 (PL 42, 1037); quoted by Thomas Aquinas, "Summa theologiae," 1, 1, 2.

6. Clement of Alexandria, "Stromata," 1, 16 (PG 8, 795); 7, 3 (PG 9, 426).

7. Origen, "Epistola ad Gregorium" (PG 11, 87-91).

8. Clement of Alexandria, "Stromata," 1,5 (PG 8, 718-719).

9. Rom. 1:20.

10. Rom. 2:14-15.

11. Gregory of Neo-Caesarea (also called Gregory

Thaumaturgus that is "the miracle worker"), "In Origenem oratio panegyrica," 6 (PG 10, 1093A).

12. Carm., 1, Iamb. 3 (PG 37, 1045A-1047A).

13. "Vita Moysis" (PG 44, 359).14. "Epistola ad Magnum,"

14 (PL 22, 667). Quadratus, Justin Irenaeus, are counted among the early Christian apologists, who devoted their works to the defense of Christian truth against the pagans.

15. "De doctrina christiana," 1, 2, 40 (PL 34, 63).

16. Wisd. 13:1.

17. Wisd. 13:5.

18. 2 Peter 1:16.

19. "Const. Dogm, de fid. Cath.," c. 3.

20. "Const. cit.," c. 4.

21. Loc. cit.

22. "Stromata," 1, 20 (PG 8, 818).

23. "Epistola ad Magnum," 2 (PL 22, 666).

24. Bulla "Apostolici regiminis."

25. "Epistola 147, ad Marcellinum," 7 (PL 33, 589).

26. "Const. Dogm. de fid. Cath.," c. 4.

27. I Cor. 1:24.

28. Col. 2:3.

29. "Epistola ad Magnum," 4 (PL 22, 667).

30. Loc. cit.

31. Tertullian, "Apologet.," 46 (PL 1, 573).

32. Lactantius, "Div. Inst.," 7, 7 (PL 6, 759).

33. Bulla "Triumphantis," an. 1588.

34. Cajetan's commentary on "Sum. theol.," IIa—IIae 148, 9. Art. 4; Leonine edit., Vol. 10, p. 174, n. 6.

35. "Constitutio 5a, data die 3 Aug. 1368," ad Cancell. Univ. Tolos.

36. "Sermo de S. Thoma."

37. Bucer.

38. Sixtus V, Bulla "Triumphantis."

39. I Peter 3:15.

40. Titus 1:9.

41. I Kings 2:3.

42. James 1: 17.

43. James 1:5.